ST ALBION
PARISH NEWS
BOOK 5

Published in Great Britain by
Private Eye Productions Ltd, 6 Carlisle Street, W1D 3BN.
© 2002 Pressdram Ltd
ISBN 1 901784 29 0
Designed by Bridget Tisdall
Printed in England by Ebenezer Baylis & Son Ltd, Worcester
2 4 6 8 10 9 7 5 3 1

Carry On Vicar!

ST ALBION PARISH NEWS
BOOK 5

Further letters from the vicar,
the Rev. A.R.P. Blair MA (Oxon)

compiled for

PRIVATE EYE

by Ian Hislop, Richard Ingrams,
Christopher Booker and Barry Fantoni

THE VICAR SPELLS IT OUT!

The Vicar's Sermon
'In Time Of War'

(as preached on the first Sunday after 9/11)

We hear a lot in the Bible about how we should all love our neighbours and turn the other cheek and blessed are the peacemakers and all that sort of stuff. Well, it may have been all very well in its time. But times have changed. Since last week we are living in a different world. How is it different, I hear you ask? Let me tell you, in one simple little word. W-A-R. And let's take that one letter at a time. 'W' (or 'Dubya' as we've come to call it!) is for 'We'. 'A' stands for 'Are'. And 'R', of course, for 'Ready', or 'Raring to go'. I am sure the children will find that easy to remember. I know I do! It's what we call an 'acro-nym' from the Greek words 'acro', meaning 'fools' and 'nym', meaning 'no one'.

And now we shall sing a special selection of hymns suitable to these stirring times in which we live.

You wouldn't find them in our 'Modern And Modern Hymn Books', because we cut them all out when I arrived here four years ago. But I have printed a special hymn sheet (sponsored by our local 'Army and Navy Surplus' shop in the High Street).

Hymns

'Onward British Soldiers'

'Stand Up, Stand Up for G. Bush'

'Old Bin Laden Lies A-Mouldering In His Cave' (to tune of 'Battle Hymn of the Republic')

Thanks to Mr de la Nougerede for this fine sketch of the vicar preaching. A.C.

ST ALBION PARISH NEWS

21st September 2001

Hullo!

And a very serious 'hullo' it is to you all this week, as some of you might have guessed who saw me at the working men's club last week, looking, I don't mind admitting it, fairly shaken.

Obviously there is only one subject that it would be appropriate for me to write about this week. One subject that shocked all of us to the core.

When something like this happens, out of the blue, we are bound to ask the very deepest questions, which go to the very foundations of our faith.

How can man behave so badly towards his fellow man?

And how does God allow it?

These are questions we must all have been asking in recent days, and I'm not going to pretend that I've got all the answers.

But all I can say is that if Mr Paddy Ashdown thinks he can get away with calling me a "smarmy git", then he's got another think coming.

I don't want to sound vindictive, but I can only say that this is one of the most outrageous and unprovoked attacks ever launched on a vicar in the long history of the church.

The Rev. Ashdown, of the United Reformed Liberal Democratic Church, has got an amazing nerve, calling a fellow church leader a "smarmy git".

I am not going to descend to his childish level of schoolboy boy abuse. Nothing whatever would be gained by coming up with similar insulting names for Mr Ashdown, such as "Paddy Pantsdown", which is what I believe his congregation used to call him.

And how, we might ask, did a man of the cloth, who lays claim to moral superiority and the right to tell other people how to live their lives, come to earn this particular nickname?

It is not my place, particularly in a parish newsletter intended for family reading, to go into the sordid details of his affair with his secretary.

Suffice it to say that the Rev. Ashdown's conduct in this matter was utterly reprehensible. If he is going to go around "casting the first stone" by calling me a "smarmy git" (whatever that is supposed to mean!), I should warn him that I have a pretty good supply of stones myself, just like the ones which in biblical times they used to throw at people who were caught in adultery.

No, I'm not going to do that. Nor will I seek to answer Mr Ashdown's ridiculous allegation that I promised to merge our two churches and make him my deputy.

Such a proposal would be highly unethical, and I would never have to put forward such a stupid idea in the first place.

Clearly retirement has not been kind to Mr Ashdown, and he should take medical advice about the problems of senile dementia, memory loss and calling me a "smarmy git".

At a time when the entire world is in a state of shock, it is pathetic that he can think of nothing better to write about.

Yours,

Tony

The Editor Writes

■ In the interests of my being able to work more closely with the Vicar, I would like to inform parishioners that I am moving into the house nextdoor to the vicarage. This will enable the Vicar to have direct access to me at all times, on a round-the-clock basis, which should greatly improve his performance and stop him coming across as "a smarmy git" (not that he does!!).

A. Campbell, Editor

PARISH COMPETITION
Set by the Vicar

Here are two pictures.
Which of them do you think shows "a smarmy git"?
Clue: The answer is B.
First winner receives a bottle of champagne.
(No *sour grapes* here Paddy!!) T.B.

AN IMPORTANT ANNOUNCEMENT FROM THE VICAR

MY FELLOW-PARISHIONERS!

At this grave time I have to announce that, as a mark of respect, we shall be severely curtailing our annual parish outing to Brighton from four days to two.

I know this will come as a disappointment to many of you, particularly those parishioners who had been planning to ask me some pretty tough questions about where I thought the parish was going.

I am thinking of our friends down at the Working Men's Club, the representatives of the Darby and Joan Action Group (such as Mr Dalyell and Mrs Castle) and, of course, Mr Ken Livingstone of the Aquatic Pets Centre.

Don't get me wrong. These people will all have a chance to say their piece in due course, say in two or three years' time.

But the point is that we are all now living in a new world and it may very well be a world in which we no longer have time for luxuries such as four-day outings to the seaside, where every troublemaker and malcontent in the parish can get up and express his opinions of the Vicar as if it was his God-given right.

It may be that I am wrong, but I never am!

So, here is the new itinerary for the trip to Brighton, which I would ask you all to cut out and pin to your fridge doors!

DAY ONE

12pm   Coach leaves for Brighton (sponsored by Stagecoach – "We'll get you there eventually")

2pm   Arrive Brighton for formal luncheon in McDonald's (sponsored by Thames Water)

3pm   Move to hotel conference room for address by the Vicar (sponsored by Dirty Des's Adult Magazine Exchange)

6pm   Vote of thanks to the Vicar, moved by Mr Campbell

7pm   Drinks party on pier (finger food sponsored by Mr Haskins of the Northern Freezer Co – "It's tastier frozen")

8pm   Prayers and community sing-song on theme of "The Last Night of the Bombs" to include Land of Hope and Glory, Rule Britannia and Jerusalem. Final rendition of The Red (White and Blue) Flag

9pm   Return to St Albion's

DAY TWO Cancelled

Tony

A VERY IMPORTANT ANNOUNCEMENT FROM MR BLUNKETT

I would inform all parishioners that a limited number of gas masks has come to light from a cupboard at the back of the Church Hall. These are being made available on a first-come, first-served basis. Apply in writing to "Gas mask Offer", c/o Mr Blunkett, The Vicarage, enclosing a photocopy of your ID card.
        D. Blunkett
        Parish Biological and Chemical Warfare Officer (formerly Neighbourhood Watch)

✝ To Remember In Your Prayers

● Mrs Short, who has been suffering from panic attacks, causing her to say things she must deeply have regretted. Let us all pray hard for Clare to be given the virtues of self-control and the realisation that no one in this world can expect to hold onto their job for ever. T.B.

✉ Parish Postbag

Dear Sir,
    How nauseating to see our vicar making a fool of himself by his shameless toadying to the Reverend Bush of the Church of Latter Day Morons. I remember when
        Yours faithfully,
        Tony Benn,
        The Old Teabag,
        Tetley Road, PGT 1PS

Dear Sir,
    I am shocked by the way I have been treated by the Vicar and his pals. After working flat out on a report on the St Albion's Cottage Hospital which is an appalling
        Mrs Claire Rayner,
        Dunagonising, Luvvie Street

Editor's Note: In view of the changed circumstances brought about by the world situation, it may in future be necessary not just to cut letters for reasons of space, but, as a mark of respect, to drop this feature altogether. After all, there are more pressing matters with which to fill the limited space available in this newsletter, such as Mr Blunkett's important announcement.
        A. Campbell, Editor-in-Chief

9

ST ALBION PARISH NEWS

The Paper That Supports Our Bombs!

19th October 2001

Oman, Thursday

Salaam! (As we Muslims say!)

As everyone will know by now, I have had to take time off from parish duties to make several missionary tours around the world to spread the gospel of war!

And what an interesting and fascinating experience it has been, to meet people of all faiths, from Father Rasputin K.G.B., of the Russian Very Orthodox Church (affectionately known to his followers as "The Butcher of Grozny") to the Rev. George Dubya Bush Jr, leader of the Church of Latter Day Morons in the USA.

But, of course, my main task of outreach has been to our Muslim brothers and sisters, with whom we share so much!

After all, are we not all the "children of Abraham" – Christians, Jews and Muslims – all fighting together to make a better world?

And let's get one thing clear. This is not a "crusade", as some people have foolishly tried to call it. Goodness me, no!

The days are gone when we in the West would send great armies across the world to slaughter innocent Muslims.

No, that was in the Middle Ages. And some of us, I'm glad to say, don't want to return to the Middle Ages, unlike Mr Bin Laden and his Muslim friends!

There's so much ignorance about Islam, isn't there? Well, let me tell you that I've been re-reading the Koran lately (the Muslim Bible), and I hope that all of you will take a copy home after Evensong next Sunday and spend a few days studying it as I (and Mr Campbell!) have been doing on the way from the airport!

And I can tell you, Islam is not what so many ignorant people believe! Islam is about peace, compassion, loving your neighbour, turning the other cheek, being kind to animals, equal rights for women, democracy, cricket, warm beards *(Surely 'beer'? A.C.)*, old ladies cycling to mosque in the early morning mist.

And, hey, aren't these the things we all believe in? Except of course for the fanatics you find in every religion, particularly Islam!

I have to say I was pretty shocked by the attitude of my Saudi hosts, when they wouldn't even let me into their country, saying that I was an "infidel" and "unclean" and that Mr Campbell and I would pollute their holy places by our presence.

Considering that I had taken the precaution of asking our accountant Mr Levy to stay at home in Israel, and told Cherie that, as a woman, it was her duty to stay at home looking after Leo for a change, I thought we would be made welcome!

In the circumstances, I can only say it was pretty un-Christian of them to refuse to see me!

But that's precisely the sort of thing I am up against in my tireless crusade to make the world a better, safer place!

All I can say is what a relief it was to address a congregation of our own British troops here in Oman, where I was able to lead them in a rousing chorus of that fine old humn "Let's kick ass"!

As I told them in my sermon, quoting from the Good Book, "Blessed are the lasting peacemakers, for they shall have to make war first, in order to make sure that the peace is in a real sense lasting" *(Book of the Apocalypse)*.

Yours,

Tony

TEXT OF THE WEEK

"Come unto me, all who are Bin Laden, and I will kill you."

Gospel of St Marksman 7.3

RECIPE OF THE WEEK: BIN LARDY CAKE

2 tbsp Best Anthrax powder
1pt Botulinus toxin
1 Can Sarin
1lb Lardy
3lb Cake

Serves 3 million people

Next Week: *Clare Shortbread*

SPECIAL VIDEO OFFER

THE VICAR'S HISTORIC SERMON AT THE BRIGHTON PARISH OUTING

Many parishioners have been asked to ask for a souvenir copy of what everyone agrees was Tony's finest sermon ever.

"THE SERMON ON THE MORAL HIGH GROUND" (PG) is now available in VIDEO and DVD versions from the Vestry at £29.99.

Now you too can thrill once again to Tony's vision of a new world where he sorts everything out – war, injustice, poverty, suffering and the single European currency.

As the organ swells to a climax, the Vicar reaches out to the hearts and minds of everyone – not just those of us in the parish, but the whole family of mankind.

REVIEWS
"More inspiring than Gladstone"
St Albion's Newsletter

"Better than Churchill"
A. Campbell

"Eat your heart out, St Francis of Assisi"
Alastair Campbell, no relation

Memo

To: PCC Members

From: Ms Jo Moore

With everyone's attention focused on the world crisis, now is a good time to announce any items of parish business that might embarrass the PCC - eg, increased expenses for members of the church council.

DO DESTROY THIS E-MAIL AND, WHATEVER YOU DO, DO NOT SEND IT TO THE PARISH MAGAZINE.

Jo

CHANGES TO LITURGY

To mark the emergence of a new world order, since Sept. 11, the following changes have been introduced to the Book of Common Blair:

New Responses

Vicar: War be with you.

Congregation: And also with you.

The congregation shall then offer each other some sign of war (it may be a punch, a slap or a kick in the ass).

Vicar: Go on, punk.

All: Make my day.

WOMEN'S GROUPS

MRS Cherie Booth gave a very interesting talk on the subject of ear acupuncture. She told us that a lot of high-flying, successful working mothers experience an abnormal degree of stress in their jobs. She passed round a small "ear needle" which, she explained, could be inserted into the upper lobe of the ear to redistribute the body's life-giving energies. The chairwoman Mrs Jowell thanked the Vicar's wife for giving up her very valuable time to provide such an interesting talk.

"We all feel very energised just by listening to you," said Mrs Jowell, "and we don't even need one of those needles when you're around."

Everyone laughed, and cakes were served by Mrs Short, who reminded the ladies that a lot of poor people in Afghanistan were dying of famine while "you are stuffing your faces with cake".

A resolution was passed that Mrs Short should not be invited to meetings of the St Albion's Women's Group again.

ST ALBION PARISH NEWS

2nd November 2001

Hullo,

And it's still a very serious "hullo", at this very dark and difficult time.

Let's not kid ourselves. This isn't a video game we're playing. This is real life. And people are going to get hurt.

And that's why it's all the more important that we should stick together, to see this thing through.

It may not be weeks. It may not be months. It may not work at all.

But that is not what matters. What matters is that we present a united front, and don't waste our energies going round, asking if it's a good idea.

We know it's a good idea. It may be a case of two steps forward, three steps back.

But "Rome wasn't built in a day" *(St. Paul's Postcard to His Mother)*. When the walls of Jericho came tumbling down, it didn't just happen overnight!

Hey, no! These things take time. Everything that's worth doing in this world takes time!

That's why it's so important that people don't go round criticising me.

I was particularly sorry to hear about the unpleasant altercation after the Service last Sunday, between young Mr Marsden and one of our sides-persons, Mrs Armstrong.

Mr Marsden had been silly enough to interrupt my sermon, when I quoted my text for the day – those very appropriate words of Our Lord, "he who is not for me is against me" *(Look, 3.2)*.

When I asked everyone to think about it for a moment, the silence was broken by Mr Marsden standing up at the back and asking whether the congregation could have a show of hands.

Very courageously, Mrs Armstrong jumped up from her pew, and wrestled Mr Marsden to the floor, gagging him with her headscarf.

When we were having coffee in the vestry afterwards, I heard several people complaining that unnecessary force had been used.

But, as I've said, this isn't a video game. People are going to get hurt, and Mr Marsden was unlucky enough to be one of the first casualties.

But then what he did, when you think about it, is the exact opposite of everything we've been fighting for. Freedom. Democracy. Openness. Tolerance. The courage to stand up and be counted in the war between good and evil. It's the old story of the sheep and the goats. And the important thing, as Our Lord made clear, is that we should all be sheep and do what the shepherd says.

And talking of what is important, surely we've got more important things on our minds than what Mrs Armstrong may or may not have said to someone who is, frankly a very insignificant member of our congregation (no disrespect to you, Paul!).

And by the same token, I was frankly shocked to hear people also gossiping about the trivial matter of our former PCC member Mr Robinson, and the £200,000 cheque he forgot to tell anyone about.

OK, this was a pretty unforgivable thing to do, and Mr Robinson was rightly dropped from the PCC just as soon as we realised what a liability he had become.

But let's get a few things straight, shall we? One, Mr Robinson was never really my friend. The PCC member he was always closest to was our treasurer Mr Brown, not me at all.

The fact that I spent my holidays in his house in Tuscany and his flat in the South of France, is neither here nor there. The truth is that he kept asking me to stay, and it would have been rude to say no.

I want to put it on the record that I never really enjoyed the six or seven holidays we spent in Mr Robinson's various homes, and I don't mind admitting that the thought often crossed my mind, as I sat by the swimming pool, being served drinks by this butler, that it

PETITION TO OUTLAW INCITEMENT OF HATRED OF RELIGIOUS FIGURES Especially Vicars

Thanks to our local artist, Mr Jolley, for this fine picture of Tony! A.C.

was odd that such a talentless man should be so incredibly rich!

The other person he used to see a lot of, of course, is our former churchwarden, Mr Mandelson, who was able to buy a luxury home in one of the most exclusive streets in the parish, because Mr Robinson lent him the money.

That was a very unfortunate misjudgement by Mr. Mandelson, for which he was quite rightly dropped from the PCC (twice!). But let's not forget also that Peter too was not even really my friend. He was much closer to Mr Brown, even though the two didn't really like each other at all, and indeed were not even on speaking terms.

But, for goodness sake, there are rather more important things going on in the world at the moment than what some rather shady car salesman got up to a long time ago (no disrespect, Geoffrey!).

As I've said a number of times now, but I can't say it too often, the message is "get real". Life is not just a video game! That's why I've written a new chorus to be sung at this week's Evensong.

> Get real, get real, get real
> > The message remains the same,
> Get real, get real, get real,
> > Life's not just a video game
> (Rcpcat)

Words and music T. Blair

Your brother (-in-arms!)

Tony

THE VICAR'S PRAYER

Hey! Go placidly amid life's ups and downs.

Look! Don't wobble when things get rough.

If you can keep your head when others are going wobbly, you'll be O.K. my son.

So walk on, walk on with hope in your heart.

Because like a Bridge over Troubled Waters (not the Wobbly Bridge obviously!)

I will keep going on until the end of the road.

Because there is a light at the end of the chunnel.

And the darkest hour is always before the dawn raid.

Amen

Millennium Tent
UPDATE

Mr Falconer writes:

The vicar has asked me to point out that the Millennium Tent is still unsold and is costing the parish £13 million to remain empty. People are still throwing their old household refuse onto the tent which the PCC has to pay the private contractors, "Team Ripoff" to clear away. This is NOT helpful and the vicar takes a very dim view of those responsible.

Thank you meanwhile for your suggestions for the Tent, including:

- *An Asylum Seekers' Holding Centre.*
- *An Eden-style Cannabis Growing Project*
- *A very silly idea about an exhibition centre to display all that's good about modern Britain. This would never work and would be an enormous waste of money, resulting in the Tent being empty for years and costing an extra £13 million. C.F.*

Peace on Earth
(At last!)

VERY special congratulations to all who have worked so hard to bring about the wonderful news from our parish mission to St Gerry's in Northern Ireland. It's taken a long time, but there is no doubt that the faith and perseverance of one person in particular has at last been rewarded.

We all know who that is. A modern-day Saint who, if anyone deserves the Nobel Peace Prize, it's him. I'm talking of course about Tony and his vision of a world free from terrorism. As he has shown in Ireland, the 'third way' is to listen, listen and listen again (the three Ls). Listen to what terrorists want and then give it to them! A.C.

Parish Highlights

Our charity quiz-night was a great success and over £27 was raised for various charities. Our editor Mr Campbell was asking the questions, and made a bit of a fool of our 'feared' local journalist Mr Paxman by catching him out with such questions as "Who is the Prime Minister of Tadjikistan?" and "How much money do you get paid?". Mr Paxman didn't know the answer to either of these questions, and we suspect that he will not be volunteering again!

In Your Garden, with David Blunkett

This is the time of year to be bringing your summer sowing of cannabis plants into the warm. 'Pot' them up (!) and make sure they get plenty of water. Come Christmas you should have a lovely crop of top-quality "grass" to celebrate the festive season in style. And this year, you can invite your family neighbourhood policeman to share your Yuletide joint. Merry "Spliffmas" to one and all!
D.B., Neighbourhood Watch

Next week: Growing poppies for fun and profit.

Hullo! (Or should it be Salaam?)

As we enter the holy season of Ramadan, our thoughts go out to all our fellow-believers across the world!

And I'm in a special position to know how they feel, since in the two weeks since I last addressed you in this newsletter I have personally flown around the world 18 times!

And let's just stop for a minute to think what that word "Ramadan" means. It is the time of year when we all prepare for the great event of Christmas.

And the real message of Ramadan is "What are we doing, and where are we going?"

And in my case we could even add "Where have you been?"

OK, I'll tell you. I've had top level multi-faith meetings with some of the top Muslims in the world, even though most of them wouldn't speak to me.

But do I look on that as a set-back? Heavens no! Or should I say "Allah be praised!"

Isn't it only by being rejected that we manage to put our message across?

OK, so Mr Assad was a little bit rude in suggesting in public that people like me should have their eyes put out and fed to the vultures. But many Muslims have a different way of showing their hospitality!

And, let me tell you, in private, it was a very different matter!

Mr Assad and I had very constructive talks, and he was particularly helpful in telling me the quickest way back to the airport.

I can tell you that my visit to Damascus made me think of another famous journey along that road!

Can any of the children tell me who I'm talking about?

No, Justin, not Mr Mandelson on his holiday. The one I'm thinking about was the great saint who "saw the light", and there, surely, is a message which is particular to us all in these dark times!

And that's what I've been trying to do, as I go round the world!

To find common ground between all the faiths in the great battle between "good" and "evil"!

And isn't that just what Harry Potter is trying to tell us?

"He who is not with me is against me" *(Book of Hogwarts 12.30)*

That is what it's all about. And that is what I've been trying to tell our Muslim friends, and everyone else for that matter. (I'm not mentioning any names obviously, but Mr Sharon will know who I mean!)

So let's hear no more of this nonsense about how I've been neglecting the parish recently, just because I've been trying to bring peace to the world!

Look, if I wasn't doing this, it is pretty likely that there wouldn't be any parish left to run, let alone for the rest of you to live in!

So, let's all think about that, shall we, as we fast through the holy month of Ramadan? And, incidentally, have you all bought your Ramadan calendars yet? They're on sale in the vestry, and all profits will go to the very exciting "Islamic Awareness Week" which is being run by Mr Brown's wife Sarah!

Your (rather jet-lagged friend)

Tony

A MESSAGE OF SUPPORT FOR THE VICAR IN ALL HE IS DOING
by Mr Prescott, who has been in charge of the parish while Tony is away

■ Tony has our unadulated support in seeking to find a way forward through the common ground to reach a position whereby all sides can be coalitioned down the middle to form a broad-band radio to achieve maximum compact within the parameters laid down for world peace which is what we are all seeking, and which can only be effected through recourse to armed confliction.

(Thanks, John, I think we've all got the idea! A.C.)

Parish Postbag

Dear Vicar,

Those of us who are old enough to remember the last World War are increasingly dismayed by your manic sermons about the desirability of starting World War Three. Your rabid and bellicose rantings in recent weeks have been

Yours sincerely,
Denis Healey, "Silly Billy",
Eyebrow Crescent

The Editor reserves the right to cut all letters from elderly parishioners of unsound mind, and furthmore to refer them to the police for prosecution under the Treason Act 1351.

✝ To Remember In Your Prayers

● Mr Byers, who has been having trouble lately with remembering some rather important facts about what he did or didn't tell the PCC. Let us pray that Stephen doesn't have to resign, but if he does, we all wish him the very best in his new job, whatever it may be! T.B.

A STATEMENT FROM CHERIE BOOTH QC

I WOULD like to issue a legal warning to Mrs Bahji Vas, proprietor and sole owner of 'Vedic Life Rays R Us', the alternative healing centre above the fish 'n' chip shop in the High Street. Although I have purchased a number of items from Mrs Vas's shop, including a traditional Gujarati bio-electric amulet to ward off carcinogenic radiation from laptop computers and a pair of inflatable holistic trousers to prevent the build-up of cellulite, I did not at any point give Mrs Vas permission to use my name as the vicar's wife to promote the business. And I hereby give notice to Mrs Vas that if she ever tries again to cash in on my status within the parish, I will bring an action against her under the Human Rights Act and she could soon find herself looking down the wrong end of a legal bill which could very easily rise to a sum in excess of £1 million.

ST ALBION PARISH NEWS

30th November 2001

Hullo!

And a pretty irritable hello it is too from your Vicar. By now most of you will have heard the rumour that Mr Brown and I have fallen out and we are not talking to each other. Thanks very much indeed to the parishioner who started this hurtful gossip which has snowballed out of all proportion. I am not going to name her, but Mrs Mowlam will know who I mean and when she examines her conscience, as we all must do from time to time (particularly her), I hope she feels suitably contrite. I also hope that she continues to take her medication and to keep away from the bottle which, I know she won't mind me saying, has been the cause of so many of her difficulties over the years.

OK, let's talk about what this is all about. Gordon and I are friends who go back a long way. And, like all real friendships, we have our ups and downs. Gordon, as he himself will admit, is not the easiest person in the world to get along with. One of his big problems, as I am sure he won't mind me pointing out to you all, is his bad temper. Everyone in the parish knows how surly he can be, often refusing to talk to anyone and sitting there morosely making everyone feel uncomfortable.

But, hey! Aren't we all like that sometimes? (Obviously I'm not, but Gordon certainly is!)

Look – friends have got to put up with this sort of thing. If Gordon is bitter, jealous and has a terrible chip on his shoulder about how popular I am in the parish then it is my duty as a friend to take it on board.

If he resents me flying around the world solving everyone's problems whilst he sits at home making a mess of the parish finances, then it could be argued that I should sack him.

But I'm not like that. I'm Gordon's friend and friends stick together, or at least they do until things get so bad that one of them has to get rid of the other one.

But, let me stress that this situation has not happened and all the rumours are just blah blah blah.

So with that dealt with, can we *please* focus on the issues that really matter – my mission of "world-building" in the new world of today.

Yours,

Tony Blah

✏ MR BROWN WRITES...

Mr Campbell has asked me to write a short note saying that the Vicar and I are great friends and that there is no rift in our relationship. I told him that I would be happy to oblige, but sadly I do not have the time, since I am very busy sorting out the parish finances. This task is not made any easier, incidentally, by people flying around the world promising the earth to everyone they meet. G.B.

A Correction

When the Vicar wrote to a parishioner recently and promised him that he would sort out all his worries about education and health and transport "toomorrow", this was a misprint. He did not of course mean to write "toomorrow" but "as soon as my new measures come on stream and the target indicators are realistically positioned." A.C.

Women's Institute

Mrs Cherie Booth gave a most interesting talk on "The Oppression of Women in Afghanistan" with slides. Mrs Booth explained how in recent years women in this primitive part of the world have not been allowed to become rich lawyers and leave their husbands at home to look after the baby. This was the reason that an invasion of Afghanistan had become necessary and she hoped that the WI would all be firmly behind her and, of course, behind the vicar who shared her point of view entirely.

A collection for the promotion of women's rights in Afghanistan was held at the end and the impressive sum of £3.74 pence was raised. Mrs Jowell proposed a vote of thanks to Ms Booth and Mrs Short seconded it "under duress". A.C.

A charming sketch of the Vicar's wife by local artist Mr de la Nougerede.

VALETE

Mrs Hunter is to leave us to take up a new job at the BP Petrol Station on St Albion's roundabout. We all wish her well in her new appointment and there are no hard feelings on my part at this scandalous betrayal. The fact that Mrs Hunter would be a complete nobody if she hadn't been lucky enough to be at school with the vicar is neither here nor there. In the current circumstances, the vicar feels it would be inappropriate to give her a farewell party or a leaving present or indeed ever to talk to her again. As it says in the Good Book, "Good Riddance to Bad Rubbish" (*Exodus 17.3*) T.B.

ALSO VALETE

Ms Margaret McDonut, one of the vicar's most loyal and helpful aides has gone to work for her friend (and mine! T.B.) Mr Desmond, the proprietor of "Dirty Des Adult Mag Emporium". We all wish her well working in Dirty Des's shop, making sure that there are plenty of brown paper bags in which to put Mr Desmond's magazines. Good luck, Margaret – we'll see you when it comes to Donation Sunday. T.B.

PARISH NOTES

There was a good turn-out for the annual Remembrance Day service when the Vicar commemorated all those who had fallen in Two World Towers. The Vicar wore an Afghan Heroin Poppy and read out the well-known lines, "At the prompting of the Sun we shall remember them".

Some of the older parishioners grumbled about how the previous wars should have got a look in but everyone else agreed it was a very moving service. The Vicar concluded, "We shall not grow old, as those on the left grow old".

The Last Second Post was played.

ST ALBION PARISH NEWS

14th December 2001

Hello,

And how gratifying it was to see so many of you at our special Memorial Meditation Service for George Harrison on Sunday. What a moving occasion that was. Not just for those of us who grew up with him, as I did as a young rock star in the 60s – but for everyone whose lives had been touched by this thoughtful, charismatic, guitar-playing spiritual teacher. As some of you have been kind enough to say, "He was a lot like you, Vicar". But let's not forget that George was part of a group, a band of disciples. And like the four evangelists, the four Beatles spread the good news, didn't they? John, Paul, George and Ringo.

"All you need is love." That was their message. Doesn't that say it all? And isn't that the whole meaning of Christmas? That's why the choir will be singing this great anthem at Midnight Mass and I'll be bringing my guitar to strum along in the background – just like George! You have been warned!

But while we're remembering all the good things that George taught us, let's not forget that sometimes George got it wrong. "Make love, not war" is fair enough in peacetime. But when you're faced with the real world and the real evil of Bin Laden or Saddam Hussein (or Mrs Filkin!) it is to another George that we must turn for enlightenment – The Reverend George Dubya Bush of the Church of the Latter Day Morons. And *his* message is "Let's kick ass" – and isn't that too the whole point of Christmas?

A Very Hare Krishna to all of you!

Tony

St Albion's Primary School

Mrs Morris Writes:

It was marvellous to see the Vicar taking such a personal interest in the school by dropping in to have his photo taken last week. He made an excellent speech about how important it was to get computers into the classroom to do all the boring old stuff that teachers used to do. Like teaching and all that sort of thing. Pupils of the future, he said, could learn directly from computers, leaving teachers free to get on with the really important job of looking for better paid employment! The Vicar's speech went down very well with the staff who all walked out in appreciation, but it was an even bigger success with the pupils who paid close attention to every word that they were text-messaging to each other on their mobiles! Great stuff, Tony. E.M.

Forthcoming Talks

We are very lucky that our former churchwarden Mr Mandelson has agreed to give a ticket-only talk, sponsored by the BP Service Station, on his recent trip to Hong Kong. He has promised us some very unusual slides of the nightlife in the famous "Pink Light" district of Wan Sum!

VALETE

Goodbye to Mrs Filkin, who was a loyal secretary at the PCC, whose job it was to check over the accounts and expenses and make sure there were no discrepancies. As you probably all know, Mrs Filkin has been under a lot of strain recently. As a result, she began to make a series of unfounded accusations against distinguished members of the PCC, such as Mr Mandelson, Mr Robinson, Mr Vaz and Dr Reid.

Her claims exhibited all the symptoms of paranoia and, needless to say, there was no element of truth in any of her wild assertions about sleaze and corruption.

Mrs Filkin has now decided to be sacked and we wish her well in her retirement. We all hope she seeks treatment for her serious mental problems – talking of which, poor Mr Marsden, it seems, is similarly afflicted and has started hallucinating. He imagines that members of the PCC physically attacked him after bellringing on Thursday. Mr Marsden would do well to seek professional help before someone goes round and beats him up – as they would be fully entitled to do, given his recent behaviour. T.B.

Parish Postbag

Dear Sir,

Parishioners may like to know that last Thursday I received a very odd call from a woman purporting to be the Vicar's wife, tellling me that I had to give her son help with his homework. Apparently, the young man was due to appear in a debate at his school Our Lady of the League Tables, proposing the motion that "This house believes in the nuclear deterrent". Could I please submit a 3000-word briefing paper on this by 9 o'clock the following morning, with key points highlighted in yellow marker. When I said that I did not regard this as part of my duties as the St Albion's Civil Defence Co-ordinator (voluntary and unpaid), the lady concerned became abusive and

Yours faithfully,
Lt Col A. Penpusher,
The Old Bunker,
Somewhere at a secret location in the parish

The editor reserves the right to shorten all letters under new anti-terrorist measures introduced by Mr Blunkett of the Neighbourhood Watch

The Vicar does his Christmas shopping. And guess what he wants for Christmas? "A dead Bin Laden!" Let's all pray for that. A.C.

WOMEN'S GROUPS

Mrs Cherie Booth continued with her weekly talks. Last Monday the subject was "Violence In The Home". As usual, it was very well attended and there was a lively question-and-answer session over coffee. The Vicar made a brief appearance at this point and asked Mrs Booth if it was not the case that women could be just as bullying as men. She told him to "shut up and sit down", which he wisely agreed to do amidst much laughter!

After a vote of thanks proposed by Mrs Jowell and seconded by everyone in the room, there was a collection in aid of The Kabul Association of Women Lawyers (Northern Alliance Branch). A.C.

The Vicar's New Year Message

A Happy New Year to you all, no matter which faith or creed to which you subscribe. As my old friend Reverend Jefferson Clinstone of the Seventh Day Fornicators put it so well in his Advent address at St Dimbleby's, "We're all of us brothers and sisters, imprisoned in our little boxes, whether we be Protestant or Catholic, Muslim or Jew, black or white, gay or straight, male or female, Liverpool Town or Arsenal United. And my message to all you good folk in Britain-land is that we've got to get out of those little boxes and get into the one great big box that's called Love." What a moving moment that was, and I know there weren't many dry eyes in that congregation at St Dimbleby's, when we joined together in that great hymn of St John of Lennon, "All you need is love."

So that's the message of this year that is now coming to an end.

It may have seemed like a year of tragedy, violence, terrorism and war. But, hey, isn't that what love is really all about? It's what the New Labour Bible calls "tough love".

And I've even written a chorus which you'll find on my website. It's a tune I've used before, but I've changed the lyrics slightly to bring it more in tune with the whole new post-September 11 mood.

> We're going to be tough, tough, tough on love,
> Tough on the causes of love
> (repeat)

Doesn't that say everything about this incredible year? I know there were a lot of you in those dark days after September 11, who thought the world was about to come to an end.

Well, all I can say to you now is, in the words of the good book, "O, ye of little faith." *(Letter to the Guardian, 7.3)*

It's a good thing that your vicar was not one of those doubting Thomases who just threw up their hands in despair and said "woe is me! There's nothing we can do. The end is nigh!"

A mere three months later it all looks very different, doesn't it? As my very good friend the Rev. Dubya Bush put it, "I come not to bring peace but to kick ass."

Wise words indeed from one of the great spiritual leaders of our time – and isn't "kicking ass" just another expression of "tough love" in action?

As it says in the Ten Commandments *(New World Order Edition)* "Though shalt kick thy neighbour's ass, and his wife's and his children's and his children's children's" *(Book of Ariel)*.

And my vision of building a new world? I know in olden times it only took three days to rebuild the temple. But sorting out the whole world in three months isn't bad! I think even our friend at the Tesco Leftover Winter Festival Puddings counter would have to agree!

So as we look forward to another year, I think we can all be modestly proud of what I have achieved!

So raise your glasses, one and all, link arms, and drink a toast with me and Cherie (and of course Euan!) to "Auld Lairg's Pisst".

Yours,

Tony

BLAIRY CHRISTMAS! Santa brings the children some wonderful presents – but the best gift of all is a visit from the vicar and his wife!

Senior Men's Fellowship Circle

MR BLUNKETT, the head of our Neighbourhood Watch, gave a most interesting talk on The Rights and Duties of the Citizen. He said there were too many "airy-fairy views" about liberty, freedom of speech and so forth. What was needed in society today was a bit of "old-fashioned discipline", especially so far as foreigners are concerned. "If people want to make their homes here," he said, "they should learn our ways." There was laughter when Mr Blunkett said that "there is no point putting up notices telling people what they can and can't do, if they can't read English".

Things turned ugly at question time, when an old gentleman in the audience asked a question about *habeas corpus*. Mr Blunkett replied that he wasn't going to stand there being insulted in fancy Latin by "toffee-nosed twits", who were only opposed to him because he went to a comprehensive. At this point Mr Blunkett stormed out, accompanied by his dog, Pierrepoint, knocking over the festive Diwali tree on the way. A.C.

Millennium Tent
UPDATE

Tremendous news to kick off the New Year! The much derided (not by me!) Millennium Tent has finally found a buyer. Messrs. Sharkey and Hutch from America, a highly respected leisure investment company, who have seen its potential as an indoor sports arena for ping pong, badminton and the like have agreed to take the Tent off our hands for the grand sum of £0.00. They have also generously agreed to build an office block on top of the church car park. So thanks to them and well done everyone! T.B

Parish Postbag

Dear Sir,

As Moderator of the United Liberal Democratic Reformed Church, I was delighted to welcome into our flock Mr Paul Marsden, a convert from your own congregation. I am only surprised that it took our new recruit so long, given the levels of intolerance, bigotry and intimidation which have now sadly become only too typical of your

Yours non-ecumenically
Rev. C. Kennedy,
536a Ashdown House,
David Steel Close

The Editor-in-Chief reserves the right to cut all letters accusing the vicar of intolerance. This is something I will not tolerate. A.C.

FROM THE VICAR'S WIFE

To whom it may concern:

In recent weeks, my client (myself), a highly important lawyer specialising in human rights, has been approached by a number of media personnel demanding to know whether Baby Leo has been or is about to be given the MMR vaccine. This is a *prima facie* contravention of Article 36(b) of the Human Rights Act, constituting a breach of privacy. Any further harassment of my client (me) will result in prosecution, followed by a lengthy custodial sentence. My client is thinking particularly here of her half-sister Miss Lauren van der Booze, who will face additional charges of treason when indicted under the act.

Cherie Booze
C/o Matrix Chambers
The High Street

ST ALBION PARISH NEWS

11th January 2002

Hullo,

And a very happy New Year to you all from India where, as some of you may know, I am on a very important mission to bring about a dialogue between the Hindu and Muslim communities.

Two great religions – but, as we all know from watching our televisions, too often they just can't seem to rub along together in a civilised way.

And yet I can already hear our friend from Tesco saying "What can *you* do about it, Vicar? It's been like that for centuries."

Well, let me remind our friend from Tesco, and everyone else who may be reading this newsletter, that they said exactly the same when I set out on my mission to bring peace to Ireland.

There too we saw two religions, two groups of people who'd hated each other for generations.

And yet now, since I explained to them the true message of 'Good Friday', the miracle has come about.

Little children can now go to school in complete safety, guarded by British soldiers!

And isn't the same thing true in Afghanistan? There too the children of Kabul can go to school under the watchful eye of our British peacekeepers (at least those kids who have managed to survive the bombing!).

And I expect I hear some of you saying, "Yes indeed, Vicar, and what about the wonderful contribution you made in bringing peace to war-torn Kosovo?"

Well, all I can say to those parishioners is, "Thank you for reminding me of that memorable achievement as well."

Look, I'm not one to blow my own trumpet, as you well know! In fact, we've had so many successes since I took over the parish in 1997 that even I sometimes forget just what a fantastic job I've done (with your encouragement, of course!).

It may seem a little bit premature to pat ourselves on the back for what I'm hoping to achieve in India!

But if our past record is anything to go by, I could understand why some of you might be thinking of putting my name forward for the next Nobel Peace Prize!

In fact, Mr Campbell tells me he's already launched a new website where parishioners can add their names to the petition which he is planning to send to the committee in Sweden which decides these things!

Let me hasten to stress that this is in no way my doing! But should you wish to add your name to all the thousands Mr Campbell has already "logged in", then please feel free to check out www.blairnobel-stalbion.co.uk!

Yours,

Tony

THE BLESSING OF THE VINDALOO

The Vicar joins in a traditional religious ceremony during his recent visit to India.

Parish Giving

An Important Announcement

Many of you have written into the vicarage in recent days asking if it is alright to put euros in the collection plate. The answer is obviously 'Yes'. If we are to play a fully active part in the modern world, it is vital that we should move with the times. So whatever you may have heard from some members of the PCC (Mr Straw will know who I am talking about!), remember that, as far as I am concerned, pounds or euros are equally welcome (whatever our treasurer Mr Brown may tell you!). T.B.

CAR PARK

MR BIRT WRITES: A year ago the Vicar asked me to make a long-term appraisal of the car parking facilities outside the church during services. My preliminary findings, following months of on-the-spot market research, suggest the following:

- There are too many cars.
- There aren't enough spaces.

There are a variety of possible solutions, which I have outlined in a 476-page working paper entitled "Towards A Solution To The Car Park Problem At St Albion's".

In brief, I suggest the following:

The setting-up of an independent 10-man task force, headed by myself, to look into the whole car parking issue and propose possible solutions (these could well involve removing the car park entirely to a more suitable location, or alternatively rebuilding the church adjacent to an already-existing car park). J.B.

Women's Group

*T*he Vicar's wife continued her series of talks with a most interesting account of the trip she and her husband had recently made to Egypt during the post-Christmas period.

Egyptians, she explained, were largely Muslims and it was part of her and her husband's present agenda to forge closer links with the Muslim community. During their visit she had met only friendship and a keen interest in her handbag, which had gone missing during a guided tour of the Sphinx.

She then showed slides of the pyramids and explained that these ancient structures were historic healing zones. Anyone, she added, could construct a pyramid at home and use it for self-help.

During questions, Mrs Short asked how a pyramid would help to cure poverty and homelessness in the Third World. Mrs Blair regretted she had no time to answer questions, owing to a prior engagement at the rectory.

Parish Postbag

Dear Sir,

As a senior member of the congregation who has seen many incumbents of the vicarage come and go, may I say that I have never known anyone so puffed up and full of himself as

Yours sincerely,
BARBARA CASTLE,
The Old Seatbelt, Harold Wilson House.

The Editor reserves the right to cut all letters just as they are about to become interesting. A.C.

ST ALBION PARISH NEWS

25th January 2002

Hullo,

And I'd like to say "It's nice to be back". But, d'you know, in a sense it isn't that nice.

And it's not just because the weather in India and Pakistan and Bangladesh and all the other places I've been to is warmer and sunnier than it is here in St Albion's!

No, it's that the people are warmer and sunnier!

Ever since Cherie and I came back from our recent world tour, we seem to have heard nothing but whingeing and petty complaints from all directions.

"Oh, Vicar, isn't it awful that my dying mother had to wait 36 hours on a hospital trolley."

"Oh, Vicar, my son's just been knifed for his mobile."

"Oh, Vicar, I've had to give up going to work because there aren't any trains."

Honestly, people will complain about anything, won't they? Haven't they got anything else to worry about?

In the countries I've just been visiting, you get a different perspective altogether, I can tell you!

They're not wasting time moaning about silly little things like trains being late and their mothers dying in hospital!

They just get on with it, in a proper Christian spirit!

If you ask me why I don't spend more time here in the parish, hey, I could reply "Who would want to, with all you lot grizzling and criticising all the time?"

But seriously, did St Paul spend his whole time in his home town of Tarsus listening to the Tarsans complaining about camel trains arriving late?

Well, he might have done, but then no one would ever have heard of him, would they?

I mean, he went everywhere! Just look at this schedule! Damascus, Thrace, Crete, Malta, Rome, Macedonia, Corinth, Tuscany! Dear me! No wonder he was so exhausted at the end of it all!

But he didn't give up! He didn't stop delivering the good news to all the peoples of the world!

Which is why I am shortly going off to Africa, as you may have read!

And what a tremendous challenge that is, this huge country with all its terrible problems – war, drought, Aids, plagues, famine!

Obviously it's not something that I can solve overnight! It might take a little while, even as long as a year!

But what kind of vicar would I be if I just sat at home in the vicarage sorting out the problems of the parish?

Haven't any of you heard of the great missionaries of history who did so much to make Africa what it is today, like Dr Livingstone? (No relation to our friend Ken from the Aquatic Pets Centre, I'm glad to say!)

And now it's my turn, to go out and take the good news to all those poor people who have never heard of the Third Way, and have to live in countries where there is no proper infrastructure, very little transport, inadequate medical services and violent crime is an everyday occurrence.

So, wish me God speed, and let's hope that when I get back, I shall see a more positive attitude from the people of this parish.

Is that too much to ask?

Tony

A POSTCARD FROM ULSTER

Thanks to all at the Mission to St Gerry's for this charming postcard. It seems to show a lovely bonfire at a street party, probably a spontaneous display of enthusiasm for the peace process which the vicar set up in Belfast and which has been such a continuing success! A.C.

PARISH ROUND-UP

AC WRITES: I wonder how many of you were lucky enough to hear the Vicar's uplifting Sunday morning interview with Mr David "Dave" Frost on the very popular radio show he runs for our local hospital, 'Off Your Trolley'? For those of you who missed it, I reprint the highlights below:

DAVE: Super to have you on the show, Vicar! Thanks for offering your services! You see, "services"? Ha, ha, ha!

VICAR: I think this morning our hearts are all going out to Prince Charles, for having to face what must be every parent's worst nightmare. As a father who's been through something very similar, with my own teenage son, I know we would all want to pay tribute to the sensitive and caring way in which I coped with this difficult problem.

DAVE: Super, Tony. That was great. And now, for all of you in the A&E Department, here's something to cheer you up – Queen's Bohemian Rhapsody..."

Parish Postbag

Dear Sir,

I was frankly flabbergasted when I heard that the Vicar had taken on Mr Birt from the TV Rental Shop to advise him on what to do about everything. Where's the Vicar been living these past few years? Doesn't he realise that this joker couldn't organise a

Yours sincerely
G. Dunwoody (Mrs)
Dunwoodin, Crewe Road

The Editor reserves the right to cut all letters that are rude about Mr Birt, for obvious reasons.

👍 THANKS 👍

*A lot of parishioners have said to me recently, "Hey, Vicar, we think **you** should be the new Archbishop of Canterbury." Obviously I'm flattered and it makes a lot of sense, but in my job you've got to learn to delegate and I've got an awful lot on my plate (see above). So thanks all of you for the letters (and e-mails!!), but we'll just have to let someone else get on with the minor jobs! T.B.*

Announcements

We were all of course delighted to hear that Mr Kennedy, the minister of the United Liberal Democratic Reformed Church, is at last planning to "tie the knot" with his long-time partner Ms *(fill in name, Alastair)*. We all hope that Charles will display a bit more loyalty to (*fill in name, Alastair*) than he has done to some of his old friends – i.e. me!! Let's also hope he won't "overdo" things on his stag night and will manage to sober up by the time he comes to say "I do" (and not "I don't mind if I do", please Charlie?). T.B.

ST ALBION PARISH NEWS

8th February 2002

Hullo!

And the first thing I want to get straight with everyone this week is all that silly parish gossip about the PCC and a certain local gas showroom run by Mr Enron Hubbard.

There is no truth whatever in all these allegations that Mr Enron was given the contract to convert the church heating system from oil to gas only because he had treated the PCC to dinner at our local Thai restaurant, the Bakhanda.

Look, there's no secret about this. He did take us out to dinner, which was very generous of him. And, yes, shortly afterwards we did give him the contract. But there was no connection between these two events, the going out to dinner and the new heating system.

The fact is that lots of people are kind enough to take members of the PCC out to dinner – Mr Ecclestone, Mr Hinduja, Mr Robinson, and many others. And it doesn't mean anything. They're not expecting any favours in return.

So let's have no more of this hurtful and pointless tittle-tattle, when we've all got much more important things to think about, like what we are to do with the church heating system which has unfortunately broken down.

And while I am on the subject of carping criticism, let me also get something else straight.

I have been accused of taking the side of our local cottage hospital doctors against a poor old lady, Mrs Addis, who had been left on a trolley covered in blood for three days.

Goodness me, nothing could be further from the truth! It's not the vicar's job to take sides, and certainly not to back our highly professional and dedicated doctors against a sad, confused, unpleasant, racist old woman!

Surely the message is that we all want better treatment for our old people. But we also want better treatment for doctors!

How do you think Our Lord would have reacted all those years ago, if he had been subjected to the kind of racist and ungrateful behaviour that we have seen recently? There might have been some very different Bible stories for our kids to learn about in Sunday School!

Yours,

Tony

Our Lord was looking around for some sick people to make better, because he had a lot of healing skills and was very good at interacting with the general public. And there was a man lying down, who was "sick of the palsy". "I've been lying here for three days," he complained, "and no one is paying any attention to me. I'm going to get my son to ring up the newspapers." And Our Lord said, "I'm sorry, no miracles for you today, my friend," and rightly went on his way.

© Rev. T. Blair 2002.

A FORMAL WARNING TO ALL PARISHIONERS

From Mrs Cherie Booth QC

I hereby give notice to all my husband's parishioners that anyone who discusses any aspect of the private life of Child E (ie, our son Euan) and in particular his plans for higher education at a college run by my friend Mr Beloff QC, President of College T at the University of O, or hereinafter suggesting undue influence, cronyism or the alleged "pulling of strings" to secure the aforesaid Child E a place at the aforesaid College T in the University of O, shall forthwith be issued with proceedings under the Human Rights 1999, with particular reference to S.51, The Rights To Privacy Of The Families Of Very Important People, and should know that this is an offence punishable by a term of not less than five years' imprisonment in Guantanamo Bay.

Signed, C. Booth,
Matrix Chambers, Hugefee Road.

Parish Postbag

Dear Sir,

I would like to make utilisation of your columns to deny catatonically all suggestions that my retiral is eminent. This is just idle and malodious tottle-tittle and I wish to nail it on the head once and for

Yours sincerely,
J. Prescott,
Working Men's Club.

The Editor reserves the right to shorten all letters denying rumours started by himself, and also not to correct the grammar and spelling of any letters which might reflect badly on the correspondent in question. A.C.

Notice

■ Whilst the Vicar is performing vital missionary work in darkest Africa, the normal arrangements as to his stand-in will apply. There will be no stand-in, as we all now accept that the Vicar is irreplaceable and anyone acting for him would be a pale shadow who might mess everything up. (No offence, John!) T.B.

'Welcome!' to our Afghan visitor Mr Khazi in his colourful native dress! The stylish Mr Khazi certainly went down a bomb with the ladies of the parish! The Vicar and Mr Khazi meanwhile had some very fruitful and interesting talks with a wide exchange of views, except obviously on the subject of Afghanistan where they agreed to differ! The Vicar says, however, that Mr Khazi has very nice manners and speaks English much better than Mr Prescott. (No offence, John! T.B.)

22nd February 2002

Hullo,

I am sure you will all have given up something for Lent!

I was determined this year to give up getting angry with people, and to try to be more tolerant and forgiving towards all those parishioners who annoy me with their stupid and unnecessary criticisms!

But I have to confess that the cynics and the moaners and the wreckers have become so vociferous that all my good Lenten resolutions have fallen on stony ground, through no fault of my own!

No sooner have we finished with all the nonsense about Mr Enron and the church heating system than the gossip-mongers and peddlars of tittle-tattle have come up with some stupid new story about my friend Mr Mittal.

And may I say first of all that he is not my friend, and I have never referred to him as such.

Indeed, when I wrote a letter to help him in his business, I was very careful to cross out the words "my friend" just in case people got the wrong idea, i.e. that he was my friend just because he had given £125,000 to help me run the parish!

I want to make it clear that there was no connection whatever between the writing of the letter and the giving of the cheque!

The vicar preaches on the text "The Wages of Spin is Death" (by local artist Mr Nougerede).

As it says in the Good Book, "It is more blessed to receive than to give." *(Revelations of St John the Major.)*

There is only one word to describe this kind of malicious slander, and that is "garbage" – from the Greek "garbos", meaning "the truth".

Has everyone forgotten what I said when I came to this parish?

I said that I had come as a new broom, to sweep away

all the sleaze and corruption which were only too familiar under my predecessors.

We don't want to go back to those days, do we, when several members of the PCC were sent to prison and the rest should have been!

Things are very different now, aren't they? We have new rules about all donations to parish funds, which I have introduced, and if it hadn't have been for those, nobody would even have heard of my friend Mr Mittal, who, incidentally, has done so much to encourage local business in the parish, even though his offices are on some island in the West Indies and he doesn't currently employ anyone in St Albion's.

So let's hear no more of this hoo-ha on stilts, shall we?

There are surely more important things for us all to be thinking about during this Lent-tide! (Or "The Pre-Easter Time Period", as Mr Birt has recommended we should call it.)

That's why if any of you have not yet given anything up, here's a suggestion for you.

Why not give up criticising the Vicar?

Yours in hope,

Tony

A Special Message To All Our English Co-Religionists from The Rev. Dubya Bush, First Church of Latter-Day Morons

"Brothers and Sisters in the Lord, I tell you the day is at hand, that day of which we read in the mighty book of the Prophet Enron, when the Great Satan shall arise, spreading his axis of evil over all the world. And note how close the word 'Satan' is to 'Saddam'. Is that a coincidence? I think not, brethren! I ask you all to join with me, along with your pastor, my good friend Rev. Blair, to take up the sword and cast out these Satanic devils as they deserve. For it is written, 'Go forth and kick ass. Thus saith the Lord.' And if he doesn't, then I do! God bless America and no one else. Here endeth the world."

LENT TALKS

✳ MRS MORRIS gave a very interesting talk on the theme of "Vocations In Today's Society". She began by saying that many children had no natural aptitude for academic subjects, and, instead of being forced to take 'A' Levels in them, just to get useless A* grades, they should be allowed to follow their vocation.

This could include such practical callings as Soap Opera Studies, the Management of Lap-Dancing Establishments, the Retailing of Sports Goods, and the Design of Mobile Phone Covers, all of which have a vital part to play in today's vibrant, skill-based, multi-cultural society. Sesame Toast and Prawn Crackers were served in honour of Chinese New Year. The two pupils from St Albion's Comprehensive who served the delicacies were awarded top grades in three modules of their Oriental Catering 'A' Level course.

✝ To Remember In Your Prayers

● Mr Vaz, who has been asked not to attend services for a month, for refusing to answer the perfectly polite question put to him by Mrs Filkin – "Is it true that you are a crook?" Let us pray that Mr Vaz is granted an early release from all the suffering he has caused us in his life, and is taken from us to a place of rest from which he will never return. T.B.

SPICE GIRL: The vicar's wife opens the biggest Cash 'n' Curry Emporium in the parish. Let's hope it doesn't get her into "a pickle" about "currying favours" and trying to "vinda-election"!

Scenes from Parish Life

Local artist Mr de la Nougerede captures the moment when an unknown man turned up at the vicarage claiming that he should take over the parish!!

Valete

We were very sorry to say goodbye to Ms Jo Moore who decided to resign at the weekend after a number of burials went wrong. It is a great shame that she is having to retire now rather than three weeks ago.

We wish her every success in her obscurity. A.C.

PARISH ENTERTAINMENT

CHURCH HALL 8.00PM
'An Evening With Mr Benn'

Mr Benn relives his long career in the parish and answers questions about how badly the vicar is running things now (4 hours 24 minutes).

Not suitable for children or adults. A.C.

ST ALBION PARISH NEWS

8th March 2002

Hullo,

It's never a pretty sight, is it, when people gang up on some member of the community just for the pleasure of seeing them being made to suffer.

When I was at school, the word we used for people like that was "bullies", and I think we all know that to be a bully is just about the worst crime that any of us can be guilty of.

Look, you don't need me to tell you who I am talking about! It's the way people have recently been treating my good friend Stephen Byers.

It was always the boy with glasses, wasn't it, who got picked on by the school bullies?

And usually it was someone who stood out from the others because he was better at his work than they were.

All this is true of Stephen, who in the past few years has literally worked his fingers to the bone on his parish work.

Never once has he complained about any of the jobs I have asked him to carry out!

He has always been there at my right hand, asking, "What can I do for you next, Vicar?"

But now this good and faithful servant of the parish (and of myself!) has been singled out for one of the most hateful campaigns of persecution that I can ever remember!

Name calling, personal abuse, even chanting that babyish old playground battle cry of the bully-boys, "Byers, Byers, your pants are on fire!"

Could anything be more beastly and horrid?

And all because Stephen openly admitted, like the transparently honest and decent person that he is, that he had been less than truthful in some of the things he has been saying about some of his colleagues at work.

But, hey, look, isn't the message here that Stephen has come clean in admitting fully and frankly to his momentary lapse?

And which of us can honestly say that we have been 100% percent truthful every hour of every day of our lives?

Obviously a vicar like myself has to be! But the rest of you are bound from time to time to stray off the straight and narrow, and you wouldn't think much of me, would you, if I were now to turn on Stephen, my friend, just because he'd lied to everybody?

So I want you all to look into your hearts and think long and hard about how you can help him at this difficult time.

The truth is that Stephen is on a journey through life, as are we all, and now and again the going is bound to become a little rough!

There will be "leaves on the line". There will be points failures. There will be delays, cancellations and even tragic accidents!

Hey, no one said it was going to be easy!

So let's get behind Stephen, and give him all the support he can! Because by helping Stephen, you are helping me, your vicar! Think about it!

Yours ever,

Tony

Mr Byers leads the prayers on Sunday. He prayed especially for the jobless in the hope that he would not soon be joining them! T.B.

HELLO, AGAIN!

For those of you who are new to the parish, let me introduce myself. I'm Peter, a very, very close friend of the Vicar and you are about to see a lot more of me. I have been on a short sabbatical, but the Vicar has now agreed that the time has come for me to return to Parish duties.

Far be it from me to criticise those who have been nominally helping the Vicar during my absence, but frankly the parish is a complete mess and it's going to need some sorting out.

Luckily, I have kept my list of names and addresses, so I know where you all live.

You are all very much looking forward to working with me again.

PETER MANDELSON

The vicar begs parishioners not to give him all the credit for the victory of the Ladies St Albion Curling Team! (By local artist Mr de la Nougerede.)

Q (sent by parishioner Tony McWalter): Could the Vicar tell us in a sentence what is his "philosophy of life"?

A: I am very glad to be given the opportunity to spell out my core beliefs. I think it is very important that people should ask this kind of question, and not feel in any way inhibited from putting to their vicar any question that they want, provided that it is asked in good faith and not to catch him out or to make him look in some way silly! I hope this answers Mr McWalter's question fully and honestly! T.B.

(This is the last of a new series in which parishioners are able to put personal questions to the Vicar on any subject they wish. A.C.)

FASHION NOTES

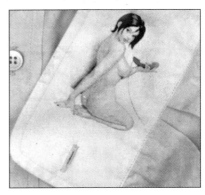

Anumber of you have noticed my new trendy pink shirt with rather racy cuffs showing a nubile young lady on the telephone! It's a gift from my new friend Mr "Dirty" Desmond of the Express Adult Mag Mart, who tells me that such amusing images are freely available on his website www.ank.co.uk T.B.

LENT TALKS

❄ We were very fortunate to welcome the Vicar to talk to us on the theme of "What To Give Up For Lent". He began by explaining that the greatest moral issue of our time was in danger of being overlooked. These days, he said, people have become obsessed with trivia and gossip. He gave some examples, such as the recent fuss over Mr Enron and the church central heating system, or Mr Mittal's gift of £125,000 to the PCC. What were silly little issues like this, he asked, compared with the moral challenge posed to our society by the overwhelming evil of foxhunting? Here was something which people could give up, not just for Lent, but for all time.

While Mrs Beckett was proposing a vote of thanks, there was an unfortunate incident involving two lady parishioners who had not been invited, Mrs Mallalieu and Mrs Hoey. Holding up a photograph of a dead chicken, they shouted that fox-hunting was the only way to rid the country of "nature's worst serial murderer". Luckily, Mr Blunkett of Neighbourhood Watch was on hand to get the two ladies arrested.

ST ALBION PARISH NEWS

22nd March 2002

Hullo,

Well, here we are, having come a long way on our Lenten journey, and it is a very good time to take stock of where we have been, and even more, where we are hoping to go to.

I think the first thing we have to do, at this stage, is to get rid of all the baggage that's going to make our journey more difficult.

What are you thinking of, Vicar? you ask. I'll tell you. We don't want any more talk of such things as Mr Mittal (who is not my friend) or Mrs Moore, or Mr Enron, or Mr Byers.

I'm going to take a leaf out of my predecessor Rev. Major's book, and draw a line under the whole lot of them!

Now, don't you already feel that things are getting better? That there's a new spirit of hope in the air?

So where do we go from here? I'll tell you! We look upwards. We look forwards and not backwards!

You see, what I'm offering you is a kind of road map to the future! We all need a road map on our journey. Otherwise you can get lost! And, hey, aren't there a lot of lost people out there? I think there are!

But a road map on its own is not much use, unless you've got someone to read that map and tell you what it's about!

And that's where I come in! Because it's my job to tell you where we're going, and how we're going to get there!

When you travel on my way (the Third Way, if you remember!), using my map, you'll find that the road leads fast and straight to the future!

You won't find any road closures, or traffic cones, or tailbacks to hold you back in the past!

What I am offering you is what I call "Phase Three" of our journey!

So what does that mean?

Let me spell it out. P-H-A-S-E T-H-R-E-E. And what does that stand for? It's obvious, isn't it?

We have had Phases One and Two, and that's what we're drawing a line under!

But, hey, I wouldn't want anyone to think that we haven't come a long way already on our journey from the past to the future!

Just remember how things used to be in the harsh and heartless days when Deaconess Thatcher ruled the roost in this parish!

Goodness me, how different it all now looks!

As I walk around the parish, I see signs everywhere of how fast things are changing in a more hopeful way!

I see daffodils springing up by the roadside! I see blossom on the trees. I see more and more women at our bus stops! I see smiling gay couples, free to walk through our streets without being gunned down!

And it all brings to mind the words of that unforgettable hymn of thanksgiving by St Satchmo, "I see trees of green, red roses too, I see them bloom for me and you, and I think to myself, it's a wonderful world"!

Isn't that a vision worth journeying towards? I'll say it is!

    Yours,

Tony

Thanks very much to Mr Mandelson for his help in compiling the above. His contribution is, as ever, invaluable and his idea about "the third phase" just shows how important it is that he returns to the team for "the third time"! T.B.

A Special Message From the Rev. Dubya Bush, Church of the Seventh Day Morons, Washington

Brothers and Sisters over there in Grand Britain! I invite y'all to join with me in the great fight against the Evil One, whoever and wherever he may be! For remember, the Devil has many guises! One minute he is hiding in a cave, like some goddamned, pesky racoon. The next minute he has a moustache and he is sitting in some palace in Baghdad. But my message is clear to him and every one of you. The U.S. Cavalry is coming! And I want y'all over there in little ol' England town to join me in our mission to kick ass in the name of the Lord. The end is nigh and it'll be a lot nigher if I have my way!
Amen and Alleluia!

The Vicar continued his series of Lenten talks last week with *"Foxhunting – The Middle Way"*

■ THERE was a very good turn-out to hear the Vicar outline his views on what he called "The most important issue facing mankind today". In the old days, he said you were either for or against hunting. But he wanted to move on from that old-fashioned polarised thinking. He proposed a Third Way, which would be neither pro nor anti, but what he called "Pranti", from the Greek "prantos" meaning "a man sitting on the fence".

This third phase in the development of the hunting debate will make everyone happy, said the Vicar.

When it came to questions afterwards, Rev. Blair said that he was very sorry but he had to catch a plane to Barcelona to see his new friend Monsignor Silvio Mussolini to discuss their continuing friendship and agreement about the "right way" to do things! A.C.

Parish Postbag

Dear Sir,

Some of us on the PCC are desperately worried at the way the Vicar seems prepared to support the belligerent and highly un-Christian views of the Rev. Dubya. If things go on like this, I for one will have no choice but to

Yours sincerely,
MRS CLARE SHORT,
The Oxfam Shop, High Street.

The editor reserves the right to cut all letters from members of the PCC who are threatening to resign because of what the Vicar's up to.

Thanks to local artist, Mr de la Nougerede, for this charming picture of the Vicar in his sponsored surplice! What a pity he has decided not to wear it any more!

ST ALBION PARISH NEWS

5th April 2002

Hullo,

That is, if I'm still allowed to say 'hullo' to people in my own parish!

Well, now I really know how Our Lord must have felt when all his followers turned against him!

One minute they were giving him a standing ovation, as he rode in triumph into St Albion's on his bicycle! The next, the crowd had turned ugly, demanding his head on a plate!

But why? Had he changed? OR HAD THEY?

That is what I want you all to think about over this Eastertide break! And, do you know, I think in my mind's eye I can see some of those who are in that crowd, their faces contorted with spite and envy!

I don't want to name names, but isn't that Mr Galloway I hear? And Mr Kilfoyle?

And what about Mr Chris Smith, once a trusted member of the PCC, and now a victim of his own bitterness and rancour?

I don't want to get personal about this, but frankly, it would do all these people a lot of good to remember what happened to Judas when he realised what an appalling mistake he had made!

I don't want to see these parishioners ending up having to go down to the local B&Q to buy a length of rope!

And listening to some of the recent talk around the parish, I even get the impression that some of you are falling into the temptation of thinking that there might be someone else who could do my job!

Well, let's just think that one through for a moment, shall we?

Let us imagine that this unknown person is somehow catapulted into the vicarage, instead of me, the rightful vicar.

He may be very competent and conscientious about some matters, such as keeping the parish accounts, making sure we don't overspend and deciding how little to give the needy or the sick.

But is that really enough to qualify such a man to take over as shepherd of the flock?

What about the quality which the Rev. Dubya Bush's father, the Rev. "Doodoo" Bush, once called, in a beautiful phrase, "The vision thing"?

Yes, "vision" (from the Greek "visios", meaning a man with his head in the clouds). And what that means is the ability to see the problems of the whole world and to find solutions for them!

I just wonder in my heart of hearts whether the imaginary person whom we're all thinking about would be capable in his dour Scottish way of lifting his head above the bean-counting towards the distant horizon from whence cometh our help.

As it says in the Good Book, "Many may be called, but only one is chosen"!

I couldn't put it more clearly myself!

Yours ever,

Tony

Roll up! Roll up! The vicar helps to make the fudge for the Easter Fayre. A.C.

Birthday Honours...

...to our late incumbent, Rev. James Callaghan, whom older parishioners still remember as "Sunny Jim". I was delighted to welcome him and Audrey back to the vicarage for a little celebration to mark his 90th birthday. Cherie made time from her very busy career to heat up her new favourite dish, Chicken Hinduja with fried rice! Everyone made lovely speeches and it was a good thing no one was tactless enough to recall how Jim's time at the vicarage ended, with rubbish piling up down the street, unburied bodies in the churchyard and rats running everywhere! And what a lesson that should be for us all today! We can see from history what happens when parishioners fail to give 101 percent support to their vicar! The vicar is forced to bow out, and the parish is condemned to 18 harsh years under the Deaconess Thatcher!

Happy 90th, Jim! T.B.

St Albion's Women's Group

We were very honoured when Mrs Kinnock took time off from her busy new life in Europe to give us a very amusing talk on "Cooking With A Microwave". She particularly singled out the TV cook Delia Smith for being "out of touch".

"The woman of today," she said, "does not have time for complicated recipes like boiling an egg." Her Neil, she said, had to go out every night to expensive restaurants in Brussels if he wanted something to eat!

There was much laughter at this quip. The Vicar's wife thanked Mrs Kinnock for her entertaining speech and agreed with her that in this modern age it was quite wrong for women to be expected to waste their time boiling eggs for their husbands or partners, when they could be out doing something useful like taking part in much-needed litigation.

There was a retiring collection for Mr Byers, who is shortly to retire.

Millennium Tent
UPDATE

Mr Falconer writes:

The Millennium Tent is still for sale, if anyone is interested. It could be used for a variety of purposes, eg a venue for pop concerts (perhaps Alastair Campbell's friend Britney might be interested?!) or a conference centre for Asian businessmen where their contribution to parish funds could be acknowledged in award ceremonies and the like.

Meanwhile, could I PLEASE ask you all to refrain from dumping your unwanted fridges on top of it. And would the owner of the burnt-out C Reg Skoda please reclaim their vehicle before Mr Blunkett of the Neighbourhood Watch has to come round and see you. C.F.

After the vicar had preached in favour of gambling, parishioners were delighted to find that he had made some new changes to the layout of the Church (by local artist Mr de la Nougerede).

Hullo,

As a mark of respect, I am leaving the first paragraph of this newsletter blank.

Now during that blank space we have all had a chance to think about the real meaning of the Queen Mother's life – what did she stand for? Not for stuffy old rituals and outmoded ceremonies, that's for sure!

No one played a more pivotal role than she did in bringing the monarchy up to date and into the 21st Century.

More than any other member of the Royal Family, she stood for change (from the Greek 'changos' meaning 'staying the same').

She was in the best sense a moderniser – someone who wanted to move things forward, to get away from the old "them and us" mentality, and to wed the whole nation together into one happy community.

Isn't that what she tried to do when she went down to the Docklands during the war, and made her famous speech "Ich bin eine Eastender". (Could you check that one please, Alastair?)

And isn't that what some of us are trying to do today?

I have been very moved in recent days by the number of parishioners who have come up to me to say "we're so sorry she's dead, vicar, but thank Heavens we've still got you to carry on her good work, with your radiant smile and your friendly wave. God bless you, sir – we hope you will live until you are 102"!

I feel very humble when I hear such sentiments expressed, because it make me realise that I am just one in a long line of popular public figures who have given their all in the service of the community!

          Yours

Tony

WINE-TASTING

Mr Lairg of our local solicitors Lairg and Co. is holding a vintage wine-tasting at his offices all next week, between the hours of 9am and 11pm. All welcome. Bring own bottle!

The vicar has been out in the parish, preaching "The Good Nukes"! (As seen by local artist Mr de la Nougerede)

Following our recent visit with the Rev. Dubya Bush of the Church of the Seventh Day Morons at his lovely home in Texas, America, Cherie and I were delighted to have this message from our kind host:

Dear Fellow-Crusader in the Holy War Against the Evil One. Laura an' I were mighty pleased to have you and your good lady Cheryl drop by at the ranch to join us in a little old-fashioned Texan hospitality. We really did have a wild time, didn't we, as we worked out how we two buddies could join hands in ridding the world of Mr Satan Hussein and those ungodly weapons of mass destruction which he has been hiding away like some pesky racoon putting his nuts in the hide of a dead buffalo. Yessir, that Great Day of Judgement is a-comin'! It's not far off now, and when the trumpet sounds and the saints go marchin' in I can tell you that we two chosen ones will be right there, shoulder to shoulder, kicking the ass of the Evil One! Glory Glory Hallelujah!

     Yours in the Lord,
Dubya, The Great Moron Tabernacle, Somewhere in Texas

A WARNING

FROM MS CHERIE BOOTH QC

The vicar's wife would like to make it clear that if there is any more malicious tittle tattle in the parish about her using the vicarage for commercial purposes in contravention of the Bar Council's Code of Professional conduct, those responsible will be prosecuted for breaching Article 23.2 of the European Charter of Human Rights concerned with "The Need to Protect the Privacy of Very Important People".

✝ To Remember In Your Prayers

● Spare a thought for poor Mrs Mowlam who is still very bitter about her dismissal from the PCC. She is going round the parish telling everyone that the vicar and his friends spread stories that she was mentally ill and incapable of doing her job. This is, of course, quite untrue and just another sad example of how mad Mrs Mowlam is and proof, if it were needed, that she was always unfit to hold down a post in the PCC. T.B.

The Flight into Egypt 2002-style

Cherie and I would like to put on record our thanks to all those who made it possible for us to take our recent pre-Easter break in Egypt. As you all know, Cherie and I have something of a struggle to survive on a vicar's stipend (even with a working wife!) and there are Euan's university fees coming up, not to mention clothes and shoes for little Leo! So we were particularly grateful to Mr and Mrs Mubarak for arranging our flight and hotel, which we could never have afforded otherwise, although we did of course donate a similar amount to charity when we got found out *(surely 'home'? A.C.)*. If anyone would like to see the video of us scuba-diving in the Red Sea and going on a camel ride round the Pyramids, this can be purchased from the Vicarage at just £28.99 (all proceeds to go to the Vicar's Egyptian Holiday Charity Fund).

Parish Postbag

Dear Vicar,

If you publish any more cosy messages from your fundamentalist friend the Rev. Dubya Bush, I for one will be forced to
Yours sincerely
Peter Kilfoyle (and 129 others)

The Editor reserves the right to cut any letters on the grounds of pathetic naïveté and reminds all the signatories of the above letter that he knows where they live.

ST ALBION PARISH NEWS

3rd May 2002

Hullo,

And I'm getting more than a little impatient with all those parishioners who keep on moaning to me about our so-called "crime wave", and how they are too terrified to come out of their homes at night.

I even had one old lady come up to me the other day, saying that she didn't dare to come to church any more because she was worried that she would be gunned down in a drive-by shooting of the type she'd been reading about in her Daily Mail!

Well, goodness me, let's get this in perspective, shall we?

Yes, there are isolated examples of crime in St Albion's, and people are rightly worried about it.

But, hey, there's nothing to worry about because I've already got it at the very top of our parish agenda (just below our local hospital and the need to recruit some teachers for the St Albion's Primary School).

Mr Blunkett of our Neighbourhood Watch has already set up a committee, with me as chairman, to take a pro-active look at the whole question of crime in modern society.

We will be asking all the key questions, such as:

1. What is crime?
2. What are the causes of crime?
3. How can we stamp it out?
4. Shall we have the coffee and biscuits now or after the meeting?

One very good idea that has come up from someone speaking off the top of their head (it was me, actually, now you ask) would be to stop handing out benefits to poor parents whose children steal money because they are poor. Think about it!

Hey, it makes a lot of sense. This is the best idea since my idea of marching yobs to the cash machine and fining them on the spot.

Anyway, I give you my solemn pledge that, by September, all crime will have been eradicated from the streets of St Albion's.

Just picture the scene: children playing hop-scotch on the village green, with no fear of being mugged for their mobile phones, old ladies cycling happily to Communion through the morning mist, with their warm beer and their fish and chips and no fear of being car-jacked.

Our friend from Tesco will tell you that this is all just a dream.

But, no, it is reality. Come September you will see for yourselves just how different things have become!

Then the cynics will have to eat their words, and realise that I am right and they are totally wrong.

To them I say, in the words of the Good Book, "O ye of little England..." *(Gospel according to Saint Look, Ch.14, v.3).*

Yours,

Tony

THE GOLDEN JUBILEE

There will be a number of events in the parish to celebrate this important anniversary next week. It is exactly five years since Tony was enthroned and I am sure that many of you will want to mark the occasion with street parties, a parade and a special service of thanksgiving to replace Sunday's normal family worship.

All of you will agree that in a changing world, Tony represents an important symbol of stability and continuity. He remains someone to look up to in today's uncertain (though much better than it was in the old days) society.

There will be a commemorative tea towel with a charming portrait of the vicar on it for those who wish to purchase a quality souvenir of the events.

Please send £50,000 to Lord Levy, c/o The Vicarage, for a set of one.

✝ To Remember In Your Prayers

● Sadly, our prayers for Mrs Mowlam do not seem to have been answered, so we'll all have to pray even harder for Mo to be given the blessed gift of being struck dumb, so bringing home to her the wickedness of her ways in pursuing a vendetta against the Vicar, just because at one time it was said that Mo was more popular in the parish than me (which is, frankly, ridiculous!). Let us pray that she is wise enough to spend the "thirty pieces of silver" she received from the St Albion's Advertiser on some good psychiatric help and not on the drink which is, sadly, more likely! T.B.

A MESSAGE FROM THE EDITOR, MR CAMPBELL

On behalf of the Vicar, I would like to make it perfectly clear that he did not in any way try to "take over" the recent funeral of Her Majesty Queen Elizabeth The Queen Mother. Had he so wished, it would have been entirely appropriate for the Vicar to conduct the entire service himself, making the address and reading all the lessons, in addition to conducting the choir and playing the organ. In fact, the Palace were very keen for the Vicar to take on the job of Queen Mother, after her sad death, but with his customary humility he suggested that the post should remain vacant for a few years, as a mark of respect to her late Majesty. Anyone who is caught making any suggestions to the contrary will be reported to the PCC (Parish Complaints Commission). A.C.

Our Treasurer's Annual Report

Unfortunately, there is no space to include Mr Brown's latest effort, but I was most amused by this picture of Gordon by local artist Mr de la Nougerede! T.B.

ST ALBION PARISH NEWS

17th May 2002

Edited by Ms Cherie Booth QC

Hullo,

And in case any of you are wondering why the vicar's wife is chairing this week's newsletter, the explanation is simple.

Firstly, Tony is far too busy on other parish business to devote his valuable time to keeping parishioners informed as to what is going on.

Secondly, it is high time that the vicar's message was written by a woman.

And, thirdly, I consider that in many ways I am better qualified than Tony to discuss a wide range of parish policy issues (as Tony would be the first to agree!).

So let me tell you what I have achieved to date.

In recent weeks I have led a number of study groups at the vicarage, under the heading "Where Are We Going And What Are We Trying To Achieve?"

Only last week I invited Mr Birt to talk to members of the PCC in his capacity as "Blue Skies Thinking Co-ordinator" on "The Way Ahead For Improving Access For Cyclists To The Church Graveyard Facility".

Mr Birt gave a very interesting lecture, with the aid of flipcharts and Powerpoint graphics, on the need to set up a suitable structure of committees to analyse and assess the available options with regard to any future developments in this context.

Another extremely useful policy meeting took place on the subject of "What does it mean to be British?"

This is a very important issue in today's multi-faith, multi-cultural, multi-gender society, and it is vital that we in St Albion's set out a template for the sort of person who defines the spirit of Britishness in a St Albion's context.

As a suitable paradigm, we looked at the example of a successful, 40-something career woman, with a young family and a husband who is a vicar working part-time.

We all agreed that such a person would be an ideal aspirational icon for the young people of St Albion's.

At question time, one of our local Asian businessmen, Mr Gotricha Hinduja, said that he would like to be British and could he have a passport?

**Cherie takes charge.
(Thanks to Mr de la
Nougerede!) T.B.**

He was seconded in this by our former Churchwarden Mr
Mandelson, who spoke very movingly on behalf of his "good
friend" Mr Hinduja, whom he assured us he had never met.

Mr Blunkett of the Neighbourhood Watch then said that there
were a lot of people who wanted to become British, but that this
was a very crowded island and was now full.

Tea and biscuits were provided by Mrs Jowell, and a vote of
thanks to myself was supported by everyone present.

I seem to be going on a bit, but I think by now you will all have
got a good idea as to just what a valuable contribution I am making
to the running of the church, even though I am not technically a
member of the PCC.

And, incidentally, I am increasingly impatient with all those other
parishioners who say that it is inappropriate for someone who has
not been elected to be given a leading role in parish policy-making.

Could I remind you all that, wearing my other hat, I am now a
judge, and would be perfectly entitled to recommend a custodial
sentence for anyone spreading such calumnies about someone
whose only motivation is to serve the parish in any way she can.

Yours threateningly,

Ms Cherie Booth QC

THE VICAR WRITES:

Thanks, Cherie, for a brilliant letter which has put all the problems of the parish in perspective! I must admit that when you first suggested taking over the newsletter, I did wonder whether there might be some objections from less forward-thinking parishioners! But Mr Campbell tells me that he has received very few letters on this subject (in the low hundreds) and has decided not to print any of them! T.B.

To Remember (Yet Again) In Your Prayers

● Sadly, our prayers for Mrs Mowlam have still not been answered! Mrs Mowlam is still with us and still, regrettably, harping on a number of imaginary grievances concerning the Vicar and her time on the PCC. Let us all pray that a meteorite from outer space may soon bring Mo's mental anguish to a swift and merciful end, and help to put the rest of us out of our misery! T.B.

VALETE

We are all desperately sad about the tragic passing away of Mrs Castle, who for many decades has been one of the most respected members of our parish. No one could dispute that in her earlier years, "Barbara", as we all knew her, made many valuable contributions to the PCC, particularly her insistence that women should play a much greater role in church affairs (no doubt she would have been very pleased to read Cherie's letter!).

Unfortunately, in her later years, Mrs Castle became somewhat deranged, becoming tragically bitter and insane (rather like Mrs Mowlam!). She even made one particularly embarrassing exhibition of herself when she accused the Vicar of being "vain, shallow, self-obsessed and without principle". Nothing, of course, could be further from the truth, as I hope our special gravestone for Mrs Castle will demonstrate. (Thanks to local artist Mr Bernie for this picture!) T.B.

HERE LIES BARBARA CASTLE — 'HER LABOUR IS TRULY OVER'

"Blessed are the goal-makers" *(Book of Clichés, 4,24.)*

The vicar meets the St Albion Footie Team and asks manager Sven if he could be picked! "We don't need another right-winger" jokes Sven! A.C.

MR CAMPBELL'S THOUGHT FOR THE WEEK

"If we say we have no spin, we deceive ourselves (although, in the circumstances, a certain amount of spin is quite understandable really)"

Book of Common Blair (as revised by A. Campbell)

ANNOUNCEMENT

MR BYERS

The vicar will not be commenting on Mr Byers at this stage due to problems with lies on the leavings (Shurely "leaves on the line" A.C.)

Hello, Churchgoers!

It's Dirty Des – your friendly Adult Entertainment Purveyor.

You are all welcome to come and peruse my wares if you fancy something a little stronger than the parish newsletter! No offence, Your Reverence!

I know that many of you support the Third World, which is why many of my lovely babes in provocative poses hail from those distant parts! Perhaps these are some immigrants Mr Blunkett should allow to stay!

Anyway, I am right behind the Vicar in his courageous action to take my cheque and put this advert in free of charge.

Dirty Des, 132 Tesco Road,
2nd Floor (ring bell),
Cash transactions only

Special discount to anyone bringing a hymn book!

ST ALBION PARISH NEWS

31st May 2002

Hullo!

I have been really saddened by the number of parishioners who have wanted to make a song and dance about the recent contribution to parish funds by a local businessman, Mr Desmond, who happens to be the owner of Dirty Des's Adult Vids and Mags Emporium in the alley behind the chip shop in our high street.

Hey, what's come over everyone? Since when was the vicar expected to take a high-and-mighty moral line on what people get up to in their business lives!

It's not my job to go round being judgmental, and laying down the law in some pious way about what people should or shouldn't do with their money!

And remember that, in this case, we are talking about what is relatively only a very small amount of money, ie £100,000, which hardly goes very far these days, as those of you may have recently tried to purchase a yacht or a football club will know only too well!

Secondly, the adult entertainment that Mr Desmond supplies is pretty harmless stuff!

Obviously, I haven't ever had any first-hand experience of the kind of thing Mr Desmond has in his shop! But Mr Campbell, who used to write for some of these magazines himself, before joining the newsletter, assures me that they are completely innocuous and give a great deal of pleasure to many parishioners, and offer employment opportunities to our ethnic minorities and to older women.

So, as we can see, there is no reason for all the innuendo down at the Britannia Arms whenever Mr Desmond's name is mentioned ("Mine's a big one" and that sort of thing!).

It's not funny and it's not clever!

But in case there is any remaining doubt over Mr Desmond's very generous gift to the parish, I have set up a completely impartial committee to vet all donations to the church, and to decide whether it is morally right for the PCC to accept them.

I am sure everyone will agree that there could be no more appropriate person to chair this committee than the man who has done more than anyone else to raise funds for the parish in recent years, my very good friend and tennis partner Mr Levy!

Mr Levy has shown that he has a real vocation for fund-raising, from donors with credentials as impeccable as Mr Mittal, Mr Ecclestone and Mr Gotricha Hinduja.

Who better to make a moral judgement on the suitability of a donation than the man who solicited that gift in the first place?

And just to make doubly sure that there are no allegations of nepotism or cronyism, I have asked my old friend Mrs Jay to serve as one of the committee. (You will remember that Mrs Jay is the Rev. Callaghan's daughter, and was the matron of our old people's home until we closed it down and threw all the old folk into the street!)

If there are any lingering doubts as to the propriety of our church-giving strategy, I would like everyone to remember those words of scripture, "It is more blessed to give than to receive" *(Gospel according to St Lucre).*

> Yours, Tony

The Millennium Tent
Great News!

The Millennium Tent has at last been sold – for nothing at all, thanks to the hard work of Lord Faulkner and his skillful negotiating team. The final offer of £0 clinched the deal against all the other offers (none).

But before we open the well-deserved champagne, there is a small matter of £200 million, which the development company, EasyBucks, has asked us to spend making the Tent accessible by road, rail, sea and helicopter.

I do hope there are not going to be any complaints about this small outlay by the parish, since EasyBucks have promised to turn the Tent into Europe's top concert venue and arts complex, as well as knocking it down and turning it into much needed luxury offices.

Can we now finally draw a line under this and would parishioners kindly remove all dumped fridges, microwaves and burned-out Vauxhall Vivas.

Thank you. T.B.

Parish Postbag

Dear Sir,

I would like to protest in the strongest possible terms at the refusal of the Vicar and his churchwardens to allow me to rejoin the congregation. I do not wish to blow my own trumpet, but I think I could contribute a lot more to the parish than a good many of the Vicar's

> *Yours sincerely,*
> *Ken Livingstone,*
> *The Newtarium*
> *(formerly the Aquatic*
> *Pet Centre),*
> *the High Street.*

Dear Sir,

I have a great deal of respect for Mr Byers, but were he to fall under a bus (which I acknowledge is unlikely, given his incompetence in running the parish bus service), I would be more than happy to step into his shoes, as I have a lifelong interest in having a high profile post. Come on, Tony! Gizza job! You gave one to Birt and he's really useless. And I'm twice as

> *Yours faithfully,*
> *Peter Mandelson,*
> *The former Churchwarden,*
> *Dunspinnin,*
> *The Herbert Morrison Estate.*

Dear Sir,

I was deeply shocked to see that the Vicar had taken money from Mr Richard Desmond, a known pornographer, who exploits Third World women in a quite sickening and

> *Yours sincerely,*
> *Ms Clare Short.*

If you have any letters on this subject to send to the Vicar, please throw them away. We would not like to hear your views, so don't join in the debate, as there isn't one. A.C.

✝ To Remember In Your Prayers

● The people of Gibraltar, who are giving such a sad example of selfishness by putting their own interests before those of their neighbours. May they be helped to realise that there is often no greater contribution we can make in this life than to give up the thing which seems most important to us, in order to make the vicar happy! T.B.

Women's Groups

Bringing The Creche Into The Courtroom

Speaker: Mrs Cherie Booth.

This is bound to be a very popular talk, touching, as it does, on one of the most important moral issues of our time. Be sure to book early for what will be an absolutely fascinating evening, which I am sure no parishioner will want to miss (and if you do, remember, I know where you all live!). T.B.

THOUGHT FOR THE DAY

*T*here is no greater temptation than to start thinking that you are more popular and successful than the person who gave you your job. Most of us know someone in our own lives who may be very close to us but secretly has thoughts of taking over our job. What such people do not realise is that being popular in this world really doesn't mean anything. Anyone can make themselves popular by giving away money, or saying things like "We've got to have better hospitals". But what good does that do? It's only talk. What really matters is not cheap popularity, but whether you're good at your job. And I think our friend Gordon knows exactly what I'm getting at here, don't you, Gordon? T.B.

ST ALBION PARISH NEWS

14th June 2002

SPECIAL JUBILEE SOUVENIR EDITION

And a truly "royal" and "loyal" hullo to you all!

What a wonderful time we've all had over the last few days celebrating the Queen's Jubilee, haven't we?

When we were planning all these celebrations a few weeks ago, I decided that it would be a good idea for me to take a bit of a back seat and let someone else take their share of the limelight for a change, i.e. Her Majesty the Queen. And all credit to her for the way she gave it her best shot!

As someone who organised the very popular celebrations we had two years ago at the Millennium Tent, I know only too well how difficult it is to make a success of events like this!

So, good for Her Majesty, for the way it all seemed to go off quite well on the day!

A number of you (quite a lot in fact!) were kind enough to say that the real highlight of the festivities was the sermon I preached at our special Jubilee thanksgiving service, kindly sponsored by local businessman Mr Desmond, the proprietor of the Adult Entertainment Emporium above the chip shop in the alley off the High Street.

For any parishioners who may have been unable to be present at the service due to the traffic building up around the church car park thanks to Mr Birt's clever new one-way system, which unfortunately created a 10-mile tailback, I am very grateful to Mr Campbell for agreeing to find room for it in this newsletter!

Yours "in jubilation"

Tony

The Vicar's wife having the time of her life at the St Albion's Parish Street Party.

THE VICAR'S JUBILEE SERMON

June 5th 2002

Today, as you all know, is a very special day. A day on which we are paying tribute to a very special lady. A lady who embodies everything that we at St Albion's believe in, and everything that I personally have always stood for throughout my ministry in the parish.

Firstly, tradition. What do we mean by that? It means having the good sense to hold onto that which is valuable from the past, and not to indulge in change for its own sake.

Secondly, heritage. This means looking backwards, not forwards all the time, and preserving, or even conserving the values that have made this country what it is today.

We think of agreeable country houses full of servants, spacious lawns where venerable old gentlemen in Panama hats are playing croquet, and beyond that the verdant acres of the age-old English countryside, where gallant huntsmen and their ladies are pursuing the evil Ken Livingstone and his gang of left-wing saboteurs who are bent on overthrowing the benign forces of conservatism and all that we in England hold most dear. God bless you, ma'am. And now we sing our final hymn, God Save The Pound.

(At this point in his address, the Vicar was so overcome by the emotion of the occasion that he had to be helped out of the pulpit by Mr Campbell, who offered him a sparkling glass of Jubilee water. Regaining his composure, the Vicar continued as follows).

Thirdly, continuity. How important it is not to sever our links with what has gone before. Surely we can learn so much from the imperishable tapestry of our nation's history? Who would wish to dismantle our great institutions? The House of Lords, the United Kingdom, the Pound, these are bastions of all that we hold most dear, and that you, ma'am, have come to embody in your gracious Self. I say this not out of deference but out of a profound reverence for your royal person, ma'am, and for your enormous popularity with which I humbly wish to be associated at this joyful time. From my wife Cherie and I, I would only wish that you have, in the words of St Delboy of Peckham, a "luvvly Jublee". And now the choir will sing the anthem 'Zadok The Vicar'.

(At this point the Vicar had to be assisted from the building, so overwhelmed was he by an onion that had miraculously appeared in his hand.) © St Albion's

■■■ Salve et Valete! ■■■

WE ARE very sad to have to say farewell to Mr Byers, who has decided to be sacked after many years and long and faithful service to the Vicar. Mr Byers was the victim of a quite unscrupulous whispering campaign by everyone in the parish, suggesting that he was no good at his job. This was wholly unfair, even if true, which makes it all the more regrettable that Mr Byers was forced to let himself go. In place of Stephen, we welcome on board Mr Darling (and no 'hullo Darling' jokes, please), who we hope will be able to sort out the mess Mr Byers has been unjustly accused of making of our parish transport arrangements.

We are also particularly pleased to welcome Mr Boateng as the first member of the PCC from the ethnic communities. Not of course that this is why he has been appointed. But I do think it shows how far St Albion's has come, when it has a vicar who's got the guts to appoint a black person to the PCC for the first time in history! T.B.

 ## To Remember
In Your Prayers

● The poor victims of the terrible Rail Disaster at Paddington. And if you can remember anything else about them (incriminating personal details, etc), please let Mr Campbell know – in complete confidence, of course! T.B.

ST ALBION PARISH NEWS

28th June 2002

In place of our normal letter from the Vicar, this week's newsletter is reprinting a transcript of the first "Open To Question" session held on the vicarage lawn and open to all parishioners who had been given tickets by Mr Campbell.

Rev. Blair: A very warm welcome to you on this lovely summer afternoon, when I know that many of you would prefer to be thinking about who's going to win tomorrow's Big Match!
If any of you guys would like to take your jackets off, please do. I'm certainly going to take off mine, as things are likely to become pretty hot over the next hour or so! Now, who's going to kick off with a really tough question?

Q: Why are you holding this "Question and Answer" session, Vicar?

A: Good question! Look, we've heard a lot about how your vicar is not being "open" about what he's doing in the parish. And what could be more open than the vicarage garden? I'm here, in front of all you guys, to give you a really straight answer to any question you guys want to ask.

Q: Is it right that the vicar's wife should go round sounding off about things which are not her responsibility?

A: Could I have the next question, please?

Q: Is this an end to spin from the vicarage?

A: Well, actually there never has been any spin from the vicarage. There has only been a perception of spin. I mean, spin is in the eye of the beholder. As it says in the Good Book, "Consider the lilies of the field. They toil not, neither do they spin." And, as far as I'm concerned, guys, what's good enough for the Good Book is good enough for your vicar.

Q: Is it true that you're going to reappoint Mr Mandelson as Churchwarden?

A: Next question.

Q: Vicar, is it true that you've done a fantastic job over the past five years?

A: Thank you, Alastair, and that seems to be a good note to end on! We'll be serving coffee and biscuits in the vicarage, and we've got some particularly fine homemade cakes bought by Mrs Jowell from Tesco! Thank you, guys, for making this occasion such a great success!

A Message from our Good Friend the Rev. Dubya Bush of the Church of the Latter-Day Morons in the USA

Brothers and Sisters in the Lord, and especially my very good friend the Rev. Tim Blair and his good lady, Shirley! I want y'all to join me on mah crusade to rid the world of evil, for once and for all. And where do we find that evil? Well, I will tell you, mah friends! In I-raq, wherever that may be. A figure with horns on his head and a big moustache, by way of name, SATAN Hussein. It's all there in the *Book of Reservations*. So that's why I put Mr Satan on notice. I am going to creep up on him and shoot him dead like the dirty rattlesnake he is. And I'm not going to give no warning, so he won't know what's coming! So, watch out, Satan. You think you're fast, but I'm faster. And if I go for my gun first, that's only because I'm shooting in self-defence. God bless y'all and God bless America.

MR BLUNKETT – A CLARIFICATION

When Mr Blunkett of our Neighbourhood Watch said that everyone on our local newspaper, the St Albion's Clarion, was "stark, staring bonkers" and should be "locked up in a looney bin for life with rats gnawing at their bones while they starve to death," he was merely indulging in a light-hearted joke and he says that anyone who suggests to the contrary is certifiably insane and should be shot.

HERE AND THERE

*T*he vicar's wife was guest of honour at a *Bring & Buy* sale held in the Church Hall in aid of Palestinian refugees, opened by the Queen of Jordan. Mrs Blair said that she was equally sorry for both sides and hoped that the conflict would soon be resolved in a sensible and peaceful way, without any further tragic loss of life. The *Bring & Buy* was a great success, raising £7.58p, mainly through the sale of home-made bombs (surely 'jams'? A.C.).

Parish Postbag

Dear Vicar,

Could I be the first to say how sorry I am to hear that you are having such a horrid time? Everyone is being thoroughly beastly to you, only because they're jealous of what a marvellous job you're doing. I know only too well the envy that attaches to someone who is so obviously head and shoulders above everyone around him, particularly when they are as second-rate and untrustworthy as Alastair Ca.

> *Yours sincerely,*
> *P. Mandelson,*
> *Hinduja Mansions,*
> *Robinson Crescent.*

The Editor reserves the right to cut any letters on the grounds that they come from Peter Mandelson. A.C.

LIFE AND DEATH

The Vicar was "devastated" by the terrible news from Japan and offers his heartfelt commiserations to all those suffering this awful loss. It has been particularly hard for the Vicar because he was hoping to welcome the St Albion football team home and give a big party at the vicarage to celebrate their victory, but this may

no longer be popular (surely "possible"?). A.C.

The Vicar Writes

We had been hoping to include in this week's Newsletter a message of support from our Treasurer Mr Brown. But, regrettably, at time of going to press we still have not heard from him. I am sure Gordon is very busy, but I would like to remind him that, as a senior member of the parish team, he shares responsibility for all the things we are doing. You can't just take credit in the good times, and then by keeping quiet in the bad times hope that you will end up being made the Vicar! T.B.

✝ To Remember In Your Prayers

● Mr Livingstone, who is having such bad luck these days with girlfriends, walls and alcohol! One cannot imagine the saintly Mr Dobson behaving in such a manner, can one? Perhaps in future people will have rather more faith in the Vicar's judgement, and will not be so quick to criticise me for excommunicating him! T.B.

ST ALBION PARISH NEWS

12th July 2002

Hullo (if that doesn't sound too 'smug'!)

I was told this week by Mr Gould that according to his researches round the parish, 62 percent of you think that is what I am – smug!

Let's just think about that, shall we? That figure means that 62 percent of you are wrong! And of course 38 percent of you are right in thinking that I am *not* smug!

So quite a few of you have got some hard thinking to do, to catch up with the 38 percent who know what they are talking about!

And even if I did happen to be smug, which I am not, wouldn't I have quite a lot to be smug about?

Let's just look at some of the things I could be very smug about if I wanted to:

1. Not being smug.

2. Really improving the quality of life for everyone in the parish in a very real way.

3. Having more women, gays and black people on the PCC than ever before. And doesn't that make a difference?

4. Introducing a whole raft of initiatives across the board in a pro-active way, to improve the quality of life for everyone in the parish.

5. Not making the same announcements twice in slightly different ways in the hope of fooling people, like some of my predecessors used to do.

So there are just a few points for you all to be thinking about.

And any of you who heard my recent question and answer session with one of my toughest critics, my good friend Mr Snow of our local Hospital radio service, know just how unsmug I can be when it comes to pointing out how well we've done!

As the extract below shows, Mr Snow really pulled no punches, which is why I thought long and hard before deciding to invite him round the vicarage to interview me:

Mr Snow: Vicar, it is tremendously good of you to give up your valuable time to explain to our listeners how successful you have been in reforming the parish since you came here in 1997.

Rev. T. Blair: That's a tough one, Jon!

Snow: I haven't asked the question yet!

TB: Sorry but, look, I know the sort of question you're going to ask, and, hey, that's your job, nothing wrong with that!

Snow: Ha, ha, ha. May I call you Tony?

TB: Certainly, Jon, you always do normally when we have dinner together!

I think that brief extract gives you all a real taste of the grilling I got from Jon. I can tell you, I knew what it must have been like for Daniel when he was thrown into that lion's den!

But I am sure that any of you who heard the interview will realise that I got the better of Mr Snow, and showed that I am in no way 'smug'.

So let's see that figure of 62 percent coming right down, shall we, when Mr Gould next goes round the parish with his clipboard!

Yours

Tony

Special Offer!!

For just £9.99 you can buy this
**SPECIAL JUBILEE
COMMEMORATIVE MUG**
to help the world's poorest.

Tony's Not Smug Mug

1p from each mug goes to
Mrs Short's "Save Africa" Appeal

Parish Postbag

Dear Vicar,

You may remember I was once married to the organist Mr Cook. In my job as district psychiatric nurse I have come to the conclusion that you, personally, are to blame for the appalling

> *Yours faithfully,*
> *Mrs Margaret Cook,*
> *Flat 57b,*
> *The Hell Fury Estate.*

The editor reserves the right to cut letters by mad menopausal women who attack the vicar in a pathetic attempt to get their own back on their ex-husbands. A.C.

✝ To Remember In Your Prayers (Again)

● Mr Livingstone, who has had another very unhappy week. As if it wasn't bad enough him being found drunk and disorderly and beating up a single soon-to-be-mother at a party, he is now single-handedly trying to wipe out the children of the parish by telling their parents not to vaccinate them against killer diseases such as MMR. Let us pray that Ken will continue to remain excommunicated from our church and punished in the hereafter! T.B.

A Message From Our Good Friend The Rev. Dubya Bush, of the Church of the Latter-Day Morons

Greetings to y'all in little old St Abigails and mah very good friend Tony Bloom. My message this week is that it's time to turn our good friends the moneylenders out of the temple. Those who worship the god Mammon have brought shame on all the decent God-fearing business folk of our land. One minute they are telling us they are our friends and showering gifts upon us, like my friend Mr N. Ron. And the next they're in gaol trying to embarrass me and to bring me down. I say to all such folks, "Get thee behind me, Satan, and thanks for all the donations. God bless America."

ST ALBION PARISH NEWS

26th July 2002

Hullo,

And thanks to all those "parish leaders" who set up our wonderfully successful 'Meet The Vicar' question-time session in the Church Hall last week.

It's all part of what I call "Doing Things Differently", and reaching out to the parish in ways which none of my predecessors would ever have dreamed of!

For those of you who haven't yet accessed the vicarage website (www.tonygreat.spinvic.uk), let me just tell you that it was a triumph!

It was probably the most constructive couple of hours that any of us in the church hall that afternoon have ever spent!

There was no cheap point-scoring! No attempt to catch me out, or make the Vicar look stupid (apart, of course, from Mrs Dunwoody, who very rudely asked me why I had given a job to my friend Mr Birt – honestly, talk about wasting everybody's time!).

In fact, now I think about it, I am not sure it was entirely wise to allow Mrs Dunwoody to attend the meeting in the first place, since we all know that her morbid obsession with trains has made her something of a laughing stock around the parish!

And Mrs Dunwoody was not the only one who, frankly, wasted everyone's time with questions that were not at all relevant or helpful!

Someone – I think it was Mr Mullin – even asked me why I was so keen to support our good friend the Rev. Dubya Bush of the Church of the Latter-Day Morons.

I told Mr Mullin that we should all be standing shoulder-to-shoulder with the Rev. Dubya in his great crusade against Satan Hussein.

As Rev. Dubya himself has put it so memorably, "Go forth and kick Satan's ass, before he kicketh yours" *(Book of the Prophet Enron, Ch. 10)*.

But apart from these rather silly interventions by people who clearly had not understood the spirit of the occasion, everyone else was agreed that it was a very useful and constructive event, which gave key opinion-formers in the parish a chance to really touch base with where the Vicar's coming from, on a whole raft of core issues which impact on the targeting and delivery of a joined-up parish agenda for the way ahead in a very real sense.

Yours, _Tony_

Women's Groups

Mrs Cherie Booth QC gave a very interesting talk on "Britain's overcrowded prisons". Too many people, she said, are being sent to prison these days, which means that there is often no room for the real culprits in our society, such as snoopy journalists and prying photographers! At question time, Mr Blunkett disrupted the proceedings by disagreeing with the speaker (perhaps not realising that she is the Vicar's wife!) and saying that in his view a lot more people should be put in prison! Mrs Morris proposed a vote of thanks and apologised for what she called the "bog standard" quality of the cakes that were served with coffee after the talk. A.C.

Announcements

Those of you who make regular donations will have noticed on your envelopes that we now ask for £24 per annum per person. This is what comes of parishioners complaining about our wealthy patrons such as Mr Robinson, Mr Ecclestone, Mr Hinduja and not forgetting Mr Desmond of the Adult Magazine Emporium in the alley behind the chip shop (ring and ask for Mr Haslum). T.B.

CHERIE IS AN OIL PAINTING!

I'm sure you're all as thrilled as I am with the new portrait of Cherie which will replace the boring old Madonna and Child in the church porch.

The picture was painted by 11-year-old Bobby Hughes, who is studying for his GCSE Art. This is very good for your first attempt, Bobby!

There will be devotional candles underneath the portrait for anyone who wishes to light one at the very reasonable cost of £30 per candle (matches extra). All proceeds to the PCC Fighting Fund, c/o The Administrator.

✝ *To Remember In Your Prayers (Again)*

● Mr Michael Foot, who is now very old and is clearly suffering from senile dementia. He has recently been going around the parish badmouthing the vicar and accusing him of being dictatorial. Let us pray that he will remember his own failings in the past and get over his bitterness at never becoming Vicar, recalling the fact that he very nearly burned the church down by being so useless! May Mr Foot make a swift recovery from his present mental condition, or, if this is not possible, may he have a merciful release and die with dignity as soon as possible. T.B.

ST ALBION PARISH NEWS

9th August 2002

Hullo,

Or perhaps I should say "bonjour", since Cherie and I and the kids are taking a well-earned break in the beautiful French village of Oubliez-la-Guerre!

And before our friend from Tesco's pipes up to ask "Who's paying for the vicar's holiday this time?", let me tell him, "Well, I suppose the answer, strictly speaking, is 'you are, matey!'".

Because that's what happens when people in the parish kick up a silly fuss about the vicar's foreign friends allowing him and his family to stay free of charge in their agreeable large houses on the continent! I have to spend my salary on holidays and end up needing a pay rise or an increased pension settlement from the parish funds!

I won't make any secret of the fact that I have been pretty upset in the past when people have carped about my family taking holiday in places like the Palazzo Fribi in Tuscany or the Chateau du Payer-Rien in the south of France.

The truth is I was only trying to save the parish money when I took up these generous offers. Honestly, that was my only motive!

And what thanks did I get for my parsimony on the parish's behalf? (From the Latin "parsimonious", meaning to "pass" the bill to someone other than "us" – look it up!)

Well, I'll tell you what thanks I got!

None at all. Just a lot of sneering and sniping from all those sad little people in the parish whose only idea of a holiday is something that they have to pay for themselves!

And although I don't want to seem obsessed with holidays, can I just nail another lie that seems to have gained hold in the Britannia Arms and the Working Men's Club over the pints of Prescott's bitter and packets of Sainsbury's GM-flavoured tomato-flavoured fish scratchings! I am not too snobby to take my holidays in Britain, as they would have you believe.

Just before we came to France, Cherie and I and the kids enjoyed a wonderful two hours driving round the Lake District on our way to Heathrow, and it was glorious!

We met some really interesting people on our visit, including some keen photographers who had somehow found out from Mr Campbell that we were visiting a place called St Bores and took the trouble to come all the way from London to join us there!

So let's hear no more about how the Vicar doesn't enjoy the real England, or the countryside!

But, as I say, I don't want to dwell on my holidays for the whole of this letter. Nevertheless, I would be failing in my duty as your vicar, if I didn't pass on what a joy it has been visiting France this summer, to use their new currency, the euro.

When one uses these new coins, one gets a real sense of people putting the past behind and marching together in a spirit of friendship and unity towards the future!

I may be on holiday, but sitting outside the village burger bar the other night, so that Leo could sample some of the local "Grand Mac et Frites à porter", I composed a new chorus which I hope we can try out at Evensong (and perhaps have a 'referendum' on whether we should add it to our permanent repertoire!).

Chorus

They've got the eu-ro-o in their hands
They've got the eu-ro-o in their hands
They've got the eu-ro-o in their hands
Isn't it time that we had too! (Repeat).

Au revoir, votre ami,

Antoine

The Vicar and Cherie hugely enjoyed the St Albion's Athletics Day held outside(!) last week and they particularly liked the Coronation anthem "Vivat Reggae" sung by all the runners at the closing ceremony to a hip-hop beat – a wonderful fusion of old and new, traditional and modern, pivotal and relevant in a very real sense. A.C.

A Notice from Mr Prescott, acting-vicar-in-charge

Since Tony has left me to run the parish in his absence on another of his jaunts round the continent, may I inform all parishioners that I have taken the following action – *viz* all areas of under-utilised open space belonging to the church, e.g. the churchyard, the bowling green, the pitch-and-putt course, the St Albion's school sports field, the convalescent garden of the St Albion's Hospice and the field behind the bus garage which we normally rent out for allotments (Gaitskell's Meadow), have all been sold to developers for much-needed low-cost housing.

Any parishioners interested in purchasing these very attractive and affordable homes, set in formerly rolling countryside, would be looking in the region of £450,000-£600,000. I would even be tempted to buy one myself, if I didn't have four homes already! J.P.

'A safe pair of Jags' (shurely 'hands'?). Mr Prescott at the helm during the vicar's absence! Thanks to local artist Mr de la Nougerede.

ST ALBION PARISH NEWS

23rd August 2002

Hullo!

As you can see, I am back at the vicarage after our very welcome family holiday in France, where we all had a chance to recharge our batteries!

It was a real pleasure to be in a place where there was no need to visit the bureau de change every time one wished to visit another country!

Not that we had any need to do so, since we were only planning to stay in France!

But just think what a timesaver it would have been, if we had been planning a trip to, say, Spain or Tuscany, if each time we came to the frontier, we had had to go to the bureau, and exchange all the contents of our wallets (or in Cherie's case, handbag) in order to change, say, francs into, say, pesetas, or lire, or whatever currency happened to be appropriate to whichever country it was that we were about to enter!

But all this has now been miraculously swept aside by the new euro which makes everything so easy!

And I couldn't help wondering, as we still had to wait in the queue to swap our antiquated pounds for this new modern currency of tomorrow, that it was an outward and visible sign of people throwing aside the prejudices of the past and joining hands as one happy human family!

I have no doubt that Our Lord himself would have been at the very forefront of the campaign to get Britain involved with this exciting experiment!

But after this vision of togetherness, I confess it was somewhat disappointing when I got home to find such a division of views in the parish over the vital need to support the great crusade against World Satanism which is being led by my very good friend, the Rev. Dubya Bush of the Church of the Latter-Day Morons.

Hey, look, I know how some of you feel about the Rev. Dubya! And sure, his style isn't mine!

A lot of what he says may not seem to make much sense!

Indeed, a lot of it may seem to be pretty mad!

In fact, a lot of you may be thinking why doesn't our vicar do more to keep him under control and generally calm things down?

But, look, don't we all of us know someone in our family or in our immediate circle who is a bit like the Rev. Dubya?

Someone who is liable to fly off the handle and threaten to declare World War Three at the drop of a hat!

Well, the last word these people want to hear is "don't"!

If you tell them that it is perhaps not such a good idea to do something, then this only helps to egg them on!

So that's why my policy with the Rev. Dubya has always been to agree with him and to support anything he proposes.

That way we've remained good friends and I hope that, by knowing when to keep silent, I have helped him to see the error of his ways!

I also hope that this will help to reassure all those fainthearts and pessimists in the parish who may be inclined to "wobble" at this time. (Mrs Short and Mr Cook may have a pretty good idea who I mean!).

Yours,

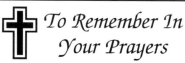

✝ To Remember In Your Prayers

● Mr Meacher, our parish "green", who made a number of quite uncalled-for and frankly idiotic attacks on the vicar and poor Mr Prescott for not taking the threat of global warming seriously enough! This is very unfair on John who is not always very quick on the uptake and has been doing his best to look after things while I have been away. *(Thanks, John!)* Let us pray that Mr Meacher makes the most of his forthcoming holiday in South Africa, and should he choose not to return, let us all wish him a happy and fulfilling retirement! T.B.

Parish Postbag

Dear Vicar,

I was disgusted to read in the local paper that the vicar is still forcing his sexual attentions on his wife, despite the fact that she is nearly 50, a mother of four and a distinguished professional woman in her own right. Once again, we see the stereotypical male enslaving his

Yours sincerely,
Germaine Greer,
The Old Belfry,
Barmy Crescent.

The Editor reserves the right to cut letters for reasons of space.

Sorry!!!

■ IN THE last newsletter, it was inadvertently stated that the vicar and his family would not this year be enjoying free hospitality while on their annual holiday. Some of you have found out that this was not strictly speaking the case. Cherie and I fully intended to pay our way at the Château Enorme, but our host, Monsieur Perrin, insisted that, since it was a private house, it would be rather ridiculous if he asked us to pay for the pleasure of staying with him!

TAR VERY MUCH! to our charming hosts M & Mme Perrin of Sunshine Cigarettes.

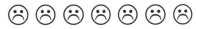

URGENT
PCC Meeting

The Vicar Writes:

People are going around saying that I am unwilling to call an "extraordinary meeting" of the PCC to discuss Rev. Dubya Bush's campaign to rid the world of Satan.

Needless to say, this is quite contrary to the truth. I have gone on record saying that I am a "listening vicar", available round-the-clock to listen to all kinds of views, however out-of-step they may be with my own thinking.

The problem arises with dates. I have, as you all know, a very busy schedule, having to catch up with all the important matters that have piled up on my desk during my brief but well-earned battery recharge.

As a result, it is with great regret that I have to say that I am unable to give any firm date for a meeting at this time. Bear with me. I am sure we can work something out in the long-term. T.B.

ST ALBION PARISH NEWS

6th September 2002

Hullo,

And this week your vicar is in the lovely city of Johannesburg in South Africa; but not, I assure you, on holiday!

I have come here with a few members of the PCC (70) to take part in a really inspiring conference which is going to end all poverty and save the planet! And there can't be anyone, surely, who wouldn't agree that this sounds like a pretty good idea!

But there are always going to be a few 'doubting Thomases' (or in Mr Porritt's case 'doubting Jonathans'!) who are ready to pour cold water on even the most well-intentioned ideas!

Mr Porritt says that your vicar hasn't been giving enough of a 'moral lead' when it comes to 'green issues'.

I gather he has even been dragging in such matters as the tarmacking over of part of the church yard to provide much needed parking space, and my decision to allow a 300 foot Orange mobile phone mast to be erected in the church tower.

He has also criticised me personally for giving pride of place at last year's Harvest Festival to Mr Sainsbury's 70-foot-long genetically modified marrow. No doubt it makes Mr Porritt feel very righteous when he accuses me of being too friendly with our local business community, but hey, get real, Jonny!

How on earth does he think we are going to wipe out world poverty by the year 2010, without the help of the people like Mr Sainsbury who create the world's wealth? It was all very well for Our Lord to tell his followers that 'the poor will always be with you', but we can do better than that in the 21st Century!

Defeatist or what? No, your vicar and like-minded souls from all around the world are here in South Africa to work

A charming traditional drawing from another local artist, Mr Cluff!

90

out how to make poor people rich without making rich people poor. Think about it!

And to mark this historic moment when we can at last look forward to a world without poverty or pollution, I have written a special chorus to be sung at this year's harvest thanksgiving.

> *'There is a green conference far away*
> *Without the Reverend Bush*
> *But he's very busy doing something else*
> *So let's not make a fuss'*

Yours 'in Gaia'

Tony

Postcard From Mr Prescott

Dear Parish
   I would just like to make one thing aboundingly clear. I am not driving out in Johannesburg in seven Mercedes, as has been repleted in certain media, e.g. the St Albion's Mercury. The number of vehicles applicated to my motorcade was only 5. So much for my so-called hippocraticness on green issues.

J. Prescott

My Greatest Mistake

An occasional series in which leading parishioners frankly and humbly confess their manifold sins and wickedness in a light-hearted way which shows them up in a good light.

THIS WEEK: **The Editor of this newsletter, Alastair Campbell**

● *My biggest mistake ever was to publish this picture of the vicar making him look like a complete idiot. He must have been furious, and I would certainly never do it again. A.C.*

Next week: **Mr Mandelson – 'My greatest mistake was to resign when I wasn't even guilty'. (Editor's note: this feature may be dropped next issue for reasons of space.)**

A Message from the Rev. Dubya of the First Church of the Latter-Day Morons

 Brothers and sisters in the Lord. All around me I hear the fainthearts chickening out of my great crusade to rid the world of the evil Satan who, even as I speak, is preparing the Armageddon for us all that was promised by the Book of Revelations. I even hear your own Minister, the Rev. Tim Blower, and his friend Mr Jake Strawberry, saying to me 'Be careful, Dubya, look before you leap. But I'm tellin' the world, I am a leaper, not a looker. Lookin' is for wimps! No offence to you, Mr Prayer, and your charming lady Cherylene. This is no time to save the world. It's time to end it. As your own great leader Mr Winston Churchyard put it so well, 'Go on Saddam, make my day'.

Rev. Dubya Bush, Moron Tabernacle, Utah

Scenes from Parish Life

The vicar orchestrating his campaign against the devil by local artist Mr de la Nougerede.

ST ALBION PARISH NEWS

20th September 2002

Howdy!

And a very sombre "hullo" it is too, as we are all still trying to come to terms with the trauma of our recent commemorative service for the tragic events of 9/11.

Many of you in the parish, I know, will find it hard to forget the anguish of sitting there, hour upon hour, watching these events being repeated on the television.

But, you know, there comes a time when you have to draw a line in the sand and move on.

And what better way to move on from this particular tragedy than to stand firm with our good friend the Rev. Dubya Bush, in his crusade to rid the world of evil.

I've heard a lot of people around the parish bad-mouthing this inspirational preacher, whom we are so fortunate to have as a friend and supporter.

To hear some people talk, you'd think that the Rev. Dubya was an idiot and a buffoon, a kind of Homer Simpson-figure from that popular TV show that Mr Campbell tells me is one of my favourite programmes.

But nothing could be further from the truth. I was recently privileged to be allowed to spend some time with him at his Texas retreat, Camp Dubya, and I have to say that it was one of the most uplifting spiritual experiences of my life!

I have never met a more intelligent, perceptive, well-informed and wise observer of our human condition, and a lot of what he says is so deep that you cannot understand it when you first hear it.

We had a prayer session round the campfire when we took as our text the great words of St John of Wayne, "a man hath got to do what a man hath got to do".

And I've really drawn tremendous strength from these comforting words, particularly when I came back home to find that in my absence almost everybody in the parish had turned against me, and were voicing all kinds of doubts and worries about where I was taking the parish.

Do you remember that bit in "High Noon" where the sheriff is trying to get the townsfolk to back him in resisting the war of terror that is about to be unleashed on their town by the moustachioed gunman with his weapons of mass-destruction?

You will remember that everyone abandoned him, because they were scared.

Well, that's what it feels like round here at the moment. But will I give up? No, because I know I'm right! It's a lonely job, wearing the vicar's badge.

But when the bad guys are out there, ready to do their worst, there is only one place for anyone who believes in the difference between right and wrong – waiting at that station, as the clock ticks round to 12 noon!

Isn't that one of the most moving scenes in scriptures? And shouldn't it be our guiding light in the dark months and years that lie ahead? And when this great crusade is finally won, what will we think then of all those members of the parish who remained quaking in their pews, when Gary Blair called them to their duty?!

I am not thinking of anyone in particular. So don't worry, Mr Brown, Mr Cook or Mrs Short, I'm not going to embarrass you!

But when next Sunday comes, I hope you'll all be joining in the new chorus I've written for Evensong, after watching "High Noon" a number of times in the private cinema of the Rev. Bush's ranch-style rectory.

"Do not forsake me, oh my Parish, etc"

Yours,

Tony

THE CHANGING FACE OF EVIL

A Homily From The Rev. Dubya Bush, of the Church of The Magnificent Seven Day Adventists

Howdy, partners, over there in li'l old Grand Britain. Courtesy of our minister, the Rev. Tommy Blower, let me say a few words about our enemy, the Evil One. Do not be fooled into thinking you know what he looks like! You do not! For the Evil One is full of guile! Yes, sir, he is! He's always changing his appearance! One minute, he has a long beard and lives in a cave. The next he has a moustache and lives in Baghdad. But underneath, we know that he is always the same Beelzebub as he ever was. As I was telling your Rev. Blower at our Bar B.Q. at the W. Ranch, the only way to deal with an Apache is to nuke him.

Another postcard from Mr Prescott at the Earth Summit

"I'm ready for when the ice cap melts,"
says Mr Prescott.

 To Remember In Your Prayers

● my poor father-in-law Mr Tony Booze who has just, with singular ill-judgement, published a book entitled *Behind The Scenes In The Vicarage: Cherie's Dad Tells It Like It Is*. Let us pray that no parishioner is foolish enough to buy this sad pack of alcohol-induced hallucinations and that Mr Booze himself may pass away peacefully in his sleep rather than bring further shame and embarrassment on his poor daughter. T.B.

 Parish Postbag

Dear Sir,
*   As people who sat through the Vicar's recent talk to the Working Men's Club, we would like to protest in the strongest possible terms about what a sickening load of bellicose*
*   Yours faithfully,*
*   B. Crow,*
*   M. Ricks,*
*   D. Spart*
*   and others,*
*   The Working Men's Club,*
*   Vic Feather Street.*

The Editor reserves the right to cut letters for reasons of space. A.C.

☺ Good News Corner!

IT'S OFFICIAL! Crime in the parish has dropped to vanishing point, exactly as the Vicar promised a year ago. Some unhelpful, elderly parishioners have told Mr Blunkett that all their houses have been burgled this week – but that's not **street crime** and that's the only type of crime the Vicar was talking about. So stop moaning and start celebrating!

Mr Blunkett, Chair of the Neighbourhood Watch

An Occasional Series

My Favourite Meal

No. 1 The Vicar

I like a lot of different types of meal from all the ethnic communities that make up our vibrantly multi-cultural parish. My ideal meal would probably begin with Prawn Crackers from Wendy Deng's Chinese takeaway in the High Street, followed by Chicken Tikka Massala from The Star of Hinduja, and then traditional British fish and chips from Cod U Like (next to Dirty Desmond's adult mag emporium). I obviously also love Scotch eggs, Welsh rarebit, Irish stew, Cornish pasties, Yorkshire pudding, Cheddar cheese and Leicestershire tiramisu. *(Please check I haven't left anyone out, will you, Alastair? T.B.)*

The vicar goes Morris Dancing – a traditional dance in which everyone hits Estelle Morris over the head for messing up the A-Level exams at St Albion's secondary school. A.C.